TRAVELLERS

CATALONIA

By
SARAH ANDREWS

Written by Sarah Andrews
Updated by Lura Seavey
Original photography by Sarah Andrews

Editing and page layout by Cambridge Publishing Management Ltd,
Unit 2, Burr Elm Court, Caldecote CB23 7NU
Series Editor: Karen Beaulah

Published by Thomas Cook Publishing
A division of Thomas Cook Tour Operations Ltd
Company Registration No. 1450464 England

PO Box 227, The Thomas Cook Business Park,
Coningsby Road, Peterborough PE3 8SB, United Kingdom
E-mail: books@thomascook.com
www.thomascookpublishing.com
Tel: +44 (0)1733 416477

ISBN: 978-1-84157-688-6

Project Editor: Sasha Heseltine
Production/DTP Editor: Steven Collins

Printed and bound in Italy by: Printer Trento.

Cover design by: Liz Lyons Design, Oxford
Front cover credits: © Thomas Cook, © Reinhard Schmid/4 Corners Images,
© Thomas Cook
Back cover credits: © Massimo Ripani/4 Corners Images, © Rudi Pigneter/
World Pictures

Contents

KEY TO MAPS

✈ Airport   ▲ Mountain

— Ancient walls   — Railway line

●ᴍ Metro station   ★ Start of walk

Introduction

Forget what you thought you knew about Spain. This is Catalonia, a land whose rich and varied history and culture are distinctly different from those in the rest of the Iberian peninsula. Once an independent kingdom, in many ways Catalonia still feels like a land apart. It has its own regional language, Catalan (see pp184–5), and unique traditions, like the gravity-defying castellers (human castle builders, see pp76–7) and fiery correfocs (fire runs, see p22).

A holiday in Catalonia can be so many things, and what you choose to do depends on the time of year and on your personal tastes and preferences. In summer, a visit to the coast is almost obligatory, but this is also a great time to walk in the cool Pyrenees mountains. Autumn and spring, when the temperatures are pleasant and the crowds manageable, are ideal sightseeing months. In winter you can ski in the Vall d'Aran or enjoy the peace and quiet of coastal towns in the low season.

Most people begin their visit to Catalonia in the capital, Barcelona, a cosmopolitan city full of life and energy. You could spend an entire holiday exploring the twisted streets of the Barri Gòtic (Gothic Quarter, *pp38–9*) or marvelling at the creative genius of Antoni Gaudí (*see pp20–21*), but beyond the city the fantastically diverse land of Catalonia tempts with its rugged coast and rolling green interior.

You don't have to stray far from Barcelona to discover the charms of rural Catalonia. The peaks of Montserrat (*see pp68–71*), one of the symbols of Catalonia, rise just 50km (31 miles) beyond the city. This is a great place to hike, and you can also visit the monastery at the top of the mountain. Near here are the vineyards of the quiet Penedès wine region (*see pp64–5*), where excellent still wines and cava (local sparkling wine) are produced in bodegas big and small.

Just south of Barcelona discover the laid-back pleasures of the Costa Daurada (Golden Coast, *pp84–5*),

where sandy shores and excellent seafood top the list of attractions. Further on is fascinating Tarragona (*see pp79–81*), Catalonia's second city, with its Roman ruins and pretty beaches. Nearby you can tour around the hills and slate-filled soils of El Priorat (*see pp86–9*), where some of Catalonia's top red wines are made. At the far southern tip of Catalonia the wild flatlands of the Delta de l'Ebre (the Ebro River Delta, *see pp92–3*) sprawl into the horizon, providing an important wildfowl habitat that's a paradise for bird watchers.

North of Barcelona stretches the Costa Brava (*pp94–5*) in all its rugged splendour. Here you'll find everything from modern resorts to 12th-century stone towns. The mix of seaside fun-in-the-sun with some of the best-preserved medieval monuments in Catalonia makes this a popular place with just about everyone, whether they be history buffs, adventure seekers or beach lovers. Though the Costa Brava has long been one of Spain's most

CATALUNYA

Catalonia, though a part of the modern Spanish state, was historically a separate country and has now regained much of its autonomy after centuries of repression (*see pp8–9*). The most obvious symbol of that autonomy is Catalan (Catalá), which has regained its status as the native language of the region (whose name in Catalan is Catalunya). Throughout this book place names and everyday phrases are given in Catalan, which is what you will see and hear everywhere, although Spanish (Castellano) is widely understood.

popular tourist destinations, it's still possible to hunt out quiet corners and off-the-beaten-track spots.

Inland, you can head towards the Pyrenees for some of the best walking country in Catalonia. The so-called 'pre-Pyrenean' regions of La Garrotxa and La Cerdanya will get you warmed up with their rolling green hills and swift rivers. As you venture further west the mountains grow more majestic, their steep peaks alternating with lush valleys where steepled churches and restaurants serving hearty local cuisine hide.

Tarragona's Roman amphitheatre has a spectacular setting

The land

Spend the morning by the shore, the afternoon in the green interior, and the evening watching the sunset over the jagged peaks of the Pyrenees. Though just over 32,000sq km (12,335sq miles), Catalonia is a land of incredible variety, and its small scale means that nothing is far from reach.

A small triangle huddling in the north-eastern corner of the Iberian peninsula, Catalonia is bordered to the east by the Mediterranean Sea, to the north by the Pyrenees mountains, to the west by the region of Aragón and to the south by the tip of Valencia. Though most of the region is hilly (the average altitude here is 700m (2,300ft) above sea level), just about every landform of the Iberian peninsula is found within its boundaries. You'll see rocky shores and sandy beaches, rugged mountains, flatter-than-flat plains and rolling hills.

The Pyrenees run nearly 200km (124 miles) along the border with France, providing some of Catalonia's most impressive scenery. Formed largely of granite, peaks here reach 3,000m (9,800ft). The tallest, the Pica d'Estats, soars 3,143m (10,312ft) high. These snow-capped mountains are dotted with small lakes popular with trout fishermen, and in spring rushing torrents of melted snow carve out trenches on the mountainsides.

The pre-Pyrenees regions surrounding Girona and Lleida are marked with rolling green hills and lush valleys. Regions like La Garrotxa are of volcanic origin, while hills elsewhere were formed by erosion of their softer rocks.

Catalonia has several other small mountain ranges too, including the dry hills of the Serra de Garraf south of Barcelona and the forest-filled Montseny, which lies just north of the city. One of Catalonia's best-known mountains is Montserrat (*see p71*), a bulbous massif created by erosion that is one of the symbols of Catalonia. Near to Barcelona, it is an excellent place for hiking and rock climbing.

Small rivers like the Noguera Ribagorçana and the Noguera Pallaresa run from the mountains down into central Catalonia, snaking their way around the area's hills. Catalonia's most important river is the Ebro, which runs down from Aragón to the Mediterranean, creating a fertile delta where rice is grown and unique bird species spend the winter.

The Mediterranean shore runs for 580km (360 miles), giving Catalonia a deserved reputation as one of the great coastal destinations of the Med. The sea is warm year-round, with a low temperature of about 10°C (50°F) and a high of around 16°C (61°F).

The city

Barcelona sits on a steady incline that runs up from the Mediterranean to the tree-filled Collserola mountains. At the base of the city are the Mediterranean port areas and the city's oldest *barrios* (neighbourhoods), such as La Ribera and the Barri Gòtic. Las Ramblas, a bustling pedestrian thoroughfare and the city's most famous boulevard, runs from the shore up to Plaça Catalunya, the heart of the city. Stretching northwest from the plaza is the modern city; the grid-like streets of L'Eixample (the Extension) fill most of the city map, while the smaller *barrios* of Gràcia, Sarrià and Pedralbes sit further from the centre.

The land

Catalonia

History and politics

Though Catalonia has formed part of Spain for a full 530 years, Catalans only grudgingly admit the fact. Most people here heed their regional government, the semi-autonomous Generalitat, much more than the far-off state government in Madrid. That attitude has caused problems and political strain for centuries.

Catalonia's independent streak comes from its heritage of having been a separate kingdom for centuries. In 988 Catalans declared independence from the Carolingian crown and began self-rule, expanding their territory exponentially and quickly becoming an important power. In 1137 the Catalan count married the heiress to Aragón's throne, uniting the two countries and paving the way for Catalonia's first Golden Age, when the kingdom of Catalonia and Aragón became one of Europe's most powerful states.

When King Fernando of Aragón married Isabel of Castilla in 1474, the nation that would be known as Spain was created, and Catalonia was tied to it from then on. From the earliest days Catalan culture and government were repressed as Spanish rulers tried to unify their new country.

In the early 18th century King Felipe V was one of the first of many rulers to try to forcefully Castilianise Catalonia. He abolished the Generalitat and banned the Catalan language. Two centuries later the dictator General Miguel Primo de Rivera, whose rule in Spain lasted a confused seven years from 1923 to 1930, tried again, outlawing autonomous rule and slamming his fist down on anything with a Catalan nationalist tinge. Most recent in Catalans' minds is the repression under General Franco, who governed Spain with an iron hand from the end of the Civil War in 1939 until his death in 1975. Franco banned the use of Catalan in public, prohibited printing in Catalan, and had all street signs changed to Castilian Spanish.

CONSTITVTIONS
Y
ALTRES DRETS
DE
CATHALVNYA,
SVPERFLVOS, CONTRARIS, Y
CORREGITS, COMPILATS EN
VIRTVT DEL CAP. DE CORT XXIIII. DE LAS
CORTS PER LA S.C.Y R. MAJESTAT DEL REY DON PHILIP
NOSTRE SENYOR CELEBRADAS EN LA VILA
DE MONTIO, ANY M.D.LXXXV.

Catalonia's rights, printed in 1704

Throughout Franco's rule, the Generalitat continued in exile, with Josep Tarradellas acting as president. When Franco died, Tarradellas returned to Catalonia, reclaiming leadership with the simple phrase, 'Ja soc aquí' ('Finally, I'm here').

When the first democratic elections were held in 1980 Jordí Pujol of the nationalist party Convergència i Unió ('Convergence and Union' – CiU) was elected the first post-Franco president of the Generalitat, a post he would hold until 2003. Meanwhile, the centrist Adolfo Suárez of the Unión del Centro Democrático led the Spanish government. During this period, the Generalitat was awarded broad control of Catalonia, with taxation rights and control over schools, police and health care.

Pujol's conservative, pro-Catalonian policies led the region smoothly from dictatorship to democracy. He tirelessly defended Catalonia's autonomy and rights as a nation, while falling just short of pushing for independence. When Pujol decided not to run in the 2003 elections, his hand-picked successor, Artur Mas, proved unable to continue his legacy. CiU lost the election to PSC (socialist) candidate Pascual Maragall, a popular former mayor of Barcelona known for bringing the Olympics to the city.

Though Maragall's socialist government received more votes than any other party it did not win a majority, forcing Maragall to form a pact with other leftist parties in order to control the Generalitat. The radically nationalist party Esquerra Republicana de Catalunya (ERC) and the green party Iniciativa per Catalunya-Els Verds (ICV) were chosen to form a three-pronged leadership system in the Generalitat. Elections in 2006 placed another, socialist, José Montilla Aguilera as President of the Generalitat, and the CiU gained a little more power in parliament.

Romulus and Remus – another reminder of Catalonia's Roman legacy

450,000 BC   Approximate date of a *Homo erectus* jaw bone found in northern French Catalonia, which means that this land has been inhabited for nearly half a million years.

12,000–500 BC   Iberian tribes from North Africa begin to populate Catalonia, leaving ruins of small settlements behind.

600 BC   An Iberian people known as the Layetanos inhabit the mountain now known as Montjuïc, in Barcelona. This is the earliest evidence of human habitation in the city.

600–500 BC   The Greeks found the cities of Empúries and Roses in La Costa Brava.

218 BC   The Romans start to take over Catalonia and the Iberian peninsula, beginning with the Greek city of Empúries. Tarraco (Tarragona) is also founded during this time.

200 BC   The first Roman road in Catalonia, the Via del Capsacosta, is built to connect the Pyrenees with Empúries and the coast. This road becomes part of the Via Augusta joining southern Spain with Rome.

100 BC approx.   Tarraco becomes the capital of the province of Hispania Citerior, the first step on its road to Roman prominence.

27–26 BC   The Roman emperor Augustus settles in Tarraco, which made it the capital of the Roman Empire for a short time.

20–15 BC   The Romans found a small settlement called Barcino, the beginnings of modern-day Barcelona.

AD 270   Barcino is attacked by Germanic barbarians invading from France,

Emperor Augustus surveys old Tarraco (Tarragona)

though the city is able to defend itself and rebuilds its walls.

415 The king of the Germanic Visigoths, Ataúlfo (Ataülf), makes Barcino the seat of his kingdom.

476 The Roman Empire falls.

711 Muslims from North Africa (the Moors) begin the invasion of the Iberian peninsula, which quickly takes them all the way to the Pyrenees.

716 Tarragona is attacked by the Mahometanos, a tribe from the southern reaches of the Iberian peninsula.

801 Barcelona is wrested out of Muslim hands by the Franks, who establish their own rule in the city.

879–97 The fabled father of Catalonia, Count Guifré el Pelós (Wilfred the Hairy), slowly draws the counties of Urgell, Cerdanya, Barcelona, Vic and Besalú into a unified region.

897 Wilfred the Hairy is killed in battle when Muslim forces attack Barcelona.

900s Catalan society begins to form; the first coins are minted, monasteries are founded and Barcelona's Romanesque cathedral is built.

988 When the Frankish Catalonian monarchy fails to aid Catalonia against the Moors, the Catalan counts declare their independence.

1054 In Barcelona, construction begins on the second cathedral, the one still standing today.

1100s The first writings in Catalan appear.

1137 Berenguer IV, Count of Barcelona, and Peronella de Aragón, the heiress of the Aragonese crown, marry, thus uniting Catalonia and Aragón.

1148 Tortosa is conquered and becomes part of Catalonia, followed by Lleida in 1149.

1213 The rule of Jaume I, 'the Conqueror', begins. Under him there is a three-pronged leadership system. The Corts Catalanes comprises military, church and popular leaders, the

Corts Generales is a representative body, and the Consell de Cent (Council of One Hundred) is an advisory body.

1229 Jaume I conquers Mallorca and in 1238 conquers Valencia, bringing them under Catalan rule.

1282 Catalan forces conquer Sicily. The Catalans are now the strongest power in the Mediterranean.

1352 The Generalitat is founded to check the power of the king, and Sant Jordí (St George) is declared the patron saint of Catalonia.

1410–12 The last Catalan king, Martin the Humane, dies without issue. Fernando de Antequera is declared king of Aragon and Catalonia.

1474 Fernando of Aragón marries Isabel of Castilla, uniting the two powerful kingdoms and creating the land that would soon be called Spain.

1516 King Carlos I declares that Catalonia cannot trade with the New World, a decree that has long-lasting effects on the region's economy until repealed in 1778.

1640–59 The War of the Segadors, when Catalonia attempts to break from Madrid in favour of French rule. Catalonia eventually decides to return to Spain and loses Rosellón and Cerdanya to France.

1701–14 The War of the Spanish Succession. Carlos of Austria and the Bourbon Felipe of Anjou both claim the Spanish throne. Felipe's troops sack Barcelona on 11 September. Bizarrely, this day becomes Catalonia's National Day.

1717 King Felipe V centralises Spain's government, stripping Catalonia of all autonomous privileges and institutions and banning the Catalan language.

1793–1814 A series of ill-fated wars between Spain and France leaves Catalonia weakened. In 1807 Napoleon's troops occupy Catalonia.

1830s The Catalan Renaissance (*Renaixença*) begins, encouraging Catalans to reclaim their cultural and political identity.

1909   Barcelona's workers rebel against the war with Morocco. A week of street skirmishes, church burnings and general chaos known as the 'Tragic Week' ensues.

1923–30   Miguel Primo de Rivera takes over as dictator of Spain. He harshly represses Catalan culture.

1931–4   Francesc Macià declares the Republic of Catalonia and Catalonia receives autonomous status within Spain. Lluís Companys becomes president of the Generalitat in 1934.

1936   Spain's Civil War begins. Catalonia opposes Franco's forces, but when the Catalan opposition becomes divided between the Anarchists and the Communists Franco takes Barcelona. Repression is widespread and thousands of Catalans are imprisoned or executed.

1939–75   During Franco's dictatorship, the Catalan language and culture are severely repressed.

The Generalitat continues in exile, with Josep Tarradellas as president.

1960s–70s   The tourist boom begins to transform the Catalan coast. Immigrants from throughout Spain flock to Catalonia seeking work.

1975   Franco dies and Prince Juan Carlos is appointed King of Spain

1977   Josep Tarradellas reinstates the Generalitat in Catalonia in October.

1980   The first democratic elections are held and Jordí Pujol is elected president of the Generalitat, a post he holds until 2003.

1992   Barcelona hosts a hugely successful Olympic Games.

2004   The socialist José Luis Rodríguez Zapatero is elected president of the Spanish government. He promises to give Catalonia more autonomy.

2006   Catalonia's Statute of Autonomy is altered, expanding the authority of the Catalan government.

Catalonia's hairy start

Wilfred the Hairy statue in Madrid

The furry founder of Catalonia, Count Guifré el Pelós (Wilfred the Hairy), is steeped in legend and has been raised to hero status in Catalan folklore. Born in the 9th century in the Catalan Pyrenees, Wilfred got his nickname from the fact that he was supposedly covered from head to toe in thick, curly hair (some legends assure that he even had hair on the soles of his feet!). Tales of his noble background, his dragon-slaying father, and his incredible strength and prowess abound, but the truth is somewhat less fantastic, though no less weighty in the minds of Catalans.

In the 800s the Franks, a Germanic people whose wide-ranging Carolingian empire was based in what is now France, ruled Catalonia, though they depended heavily on the local counts for imposing order. Wilfred was one such count, though he was decidedly more enterprising than most. With the help of his brother, he began the systematic takeover of one Catalan region after another, wresting power from the disliked Frankish nobleman who held official control in the area and taking it for himself, all the while making sure to declare his loyalty to the Carolingian crown so that he wouldn't incur the anger of the king in France.

Slowly, the hairy hero was creating a new land. He centred the governance of his territory in Barcelona, making the city the capital of the newly formed region of Catalonia. Though Catalonia wouldn't declare its independence from the Carolingian crown until more than a century later, the groundwork was being laid for the establishment of a unified country.

According to legend, Wilfred the Hairy also bequeathed to Catalonia

'La Senyera', the Catalan flag. The story says that Wilfred was mortally wounded in a battle with Muslim troops who were trying to take Barcelona. At this time, rather ironically, he was officially in the service of his overlord Charles 'the Bald'. When Wilfred fell, Charles noticed that his vassal's shield was unadorned. So he dipped his fingers in Wilfred's blood and smeared them on his blank golden shield, creating the four red stripes on gold of the Catalan flag.

The fact that so many glorious stories about Wilfred have survived can be traced to the count's heavy support of the Church. He dedicated a sizeable portion of his fortune to the foundation and support of monasteries and convents throughout the Catalan territory, winning the unending devotion of the monks,

The Catalan flag is one of Wilfred the Hairy's legacies – or so legend would have it

Wilfred the Hairy's tomb in the monastery of Santa Maria de Ripoll, which he founded

who wrote most of the histories in those days. To thank Wilfred the Hairy for his devotion to the Church, the monastery scribes penned eloquent tales of Wilfred's bravery and strength. They also invented a background worthy of a hero by creating a detailed story of how the count's father killed an evil dragon with a tree branch. Through the years, the tale of Wilfred's father was mixed with stories of the hairy leader's own glorious acts, and today you can see a 14th-century carving on Barcelona's cathedral that shows an exceptionally hairy man beating a small dragon with a tree branch. You'll spot the carving high above the portal of Sant Iu (Saint Ivo) on the Carrer dels Comtes, on the side of the cathedral.

Culture

With the Mediterranean Sea providing a swinging door for new ideas, and the French border lying just across the Pyrenees, Catalonia has always been Spain's most 'European' region. That openness is seen constantly in the region's art and culture.

Art

Early days

Catalonia is now known as an artistic hotspot, but it got off to a slow start. There is little ancient art to speak of, aside from a few scattered examples of rock and cave art and a selection of Roman sculptures and mosaics on display in museums like Tarragona's Museu d'Arqueologia (Museum of Archaeology). Catalonia's medieval art, which originally hung in chapels and monasteries in the Catalan countryside, is abundant but not particularly innovative. The best pieces were long ago taken from the Church and displayed in museums in Barcelona or elsewhere.

The 20th century

While the 18th and 19th centuries were decidedly unexciting times for the art world here, the 20th century finally brought exciting styles and artists. Modernist painters like Ramón Casas and Santiago Rusiñol came on the scene at the turn of the century, painting landscapes and everyday scenes that relied heavily on the use of natural light and bright colours. For a time these painters worked with a young upstart called Pablo Picasso. In fact, they gave the Malaga native the chance to put on his first solo exhibition in their Barcelona tavern, Els Quatre Gats (*see p53*).

Picasso eventually moved to Paris, where he would live for much of his

OF BATS AND DRAGONS: LEGENDARY MODERNISTS

On many Modernist constructions, including the ornate streetlights on Barcelona's Passeig de Gràcia and Gaudí's Palau Güell, you'll spot the images of small bats and ferocious-looking dragons. What seems like a homage to fantasy novels is really a reference to Catalan folklore. The bat was the symbol of the great King Jaume I, who gave a bat credit for alerting him to an enemy's presence and thus saving his life. The dragon gives a nod to Catalonia's patron saint, Sant Jordi (St George), who supposedly saved the land when he slew a dragon.

career, but in Barcelona another gifted painter, Joan Miró, was developing. Miró was born and raised in the Barri Gótic, and Catalan culture heavily shaped his work. He, too, left for Paris at an early age but in later life wound up working on the Catalan-speaking island of Mallorca.

Salvador Dalí, yet another Catalan son, was born in Figueres, north of Barcelona near the French border. Throughout his life the moustached master of surrealism and self-promotion would have a special tie to Catalonia, and images of the Costa Brava, where he lived for many years, appear in countless works.

Perhaps Catalonia's greatest living artist is Antonio Tàpies, whose foundation in Barcelona is an excellent place to see modern art. Also look out for other notable names like Albert Ràfols Casamada, Josep Maria Subirachs (who is in charge of the design on La Sagrada Familia) and Susana Solano.

Architecture

Though the most famous architectural style to emerge from Catalonia is Modernism, with Antoni Gaudí at the head, the region is also home to some of the best Romanesque and Gothic architecture in Europe, much of it seen in the churches and monasteries in small towns and rural regions.

Romanesque

The small towns of the Catalan Pyrenees are filled with small stone churches built in the Romanesque style, making Catalonia one of the best regions in Europe to see this kind of architecture. *See more on pp130–31.*

Romanesque painting in the monastery of Ripoll

Catalan Gothic

Catalonia's 13th-century Golden Age saw the best of Catalonia's medieval architecture, Catalan Gothic. A simpler, more pure version of French Gothic, the Catalan version relies on straight, delicate lines and minimal decoration to create elegant buildings. One of the best examples of Catalan Gothic is the Santa María del Mar Basilica (*see pp46–7*) in Barcelona, but other excellent examples of the style are found in the monasteries of Poblet and Santes Creus (*see pp 120–21*) and in the cathedrals of Tarragona (*see pp79–81*) and Girona (*see pp95–7*).

Modernisme

See pp52–3.

Contemporary

Catalonia is brimming over with innovative new designs, most of them in or around Barcelona. Highlights include the soaring tower by French architect Jean Nouvel, built in the Plaça de Glòries in northern Barcelona, and a triangular conference centre built for the Forum 2004. Also look out for British architect Richard Rogers' shopping centre near Plaça Espanya, a circular building converted from an old bullring.

Literature

Catalan authors have never had the international acclaim of Castilian writers such as Miguel Cervantes, Federico García Lorca or Camilo José

The simplicity of Catalan Gothic is exemplified in Barcelona's Santa María del Mar

Cela, but the region has produced some notable works. Catalan literature first appeared in the 12th century with examples of light love poems written for the court. Catalonia's first renowned writer, Ramon Llull (1233–1315), would appear on the scene nearly a century later, establishing his place in history by writing in the vernacular.

Early Catalan literature saw its heyday in the 15th century with writers like Ausiàs March, who became Catalonia's first revered poet. At this time Joanot Martorell's *Tirant lo Blanc*, supposedly Cervantes' favourite novel, was also published.

The next literary boom came in the late 19th century in the so-called Catalan Renaissance, when writers and artists alike looked to the glory of Catalonia's past for inspiration. Great writers of this time included the clergyman Jacint Verdaguer and Modernist writer Joan Maragall. Great 20th-century writers include Mercé Rodoreda, whose *Plaça del Diamant* is a poignant story of a woman's survival during the Civil War in Barcelona, and Josep Pla, whose incredibly prolific pen led him to write dozens of books on everything from politics to poetry. Catalan contemporary writers have a strong tendency to reflect on the past rather than write about present happenings; Eduardo Mendoza's *Ciudad de los Prodigios* (City of Marvels) looks at late-19th-century Barcelona, and Carlos Ruiz Zafón's bestseller *La Sombra del Viento* (The Shadow of the Wind) is also set in Barcelona, in the period before the Civil War.

Language

Though nearly everyone in Catalonia speaks Castellano (Spanish), the heart and soul of the land can only be expressed in its own language, Catalan. A Romance language, not merely a dialect, Catalan developed from Latin alongside Spanish, French and other languages. The differences between Catalan and Spanish can be traced to the differences in the Latin spoken by Romans in southern Iberia, who were by and large educated and spoke old Latin, and the Latin spoken by those in northern Iberia, who spoke a less formal Latin full of slang and new words.

A page from *Tirant lo Blanc*, the 1490 epic romance which greatly influenced Cervantes

Antoni Gaudí, Modernist genius

He built spiral staircases that imitate snails' shells and columns shaped like human bones. He made blue mosaics that shimmer like the Mediterranean and ceiling beams that look like tree trunks. Architect Antoni Gaudí was innovative, to say the least, and his creations are some of Catalonia's greatest possessions.

Born to a middle-class family in Reus, near Tarragona, Antoni Gaudí was dubbed an eccentric from an early age, and not without reason. While other architects were designing sensible iron balconies and standard rectangular apartment blocks, Gaudí set out to build fantastical buildings inspired by nature. His façades were swirling, undulating faces that hid interiors full of colourful glass and mosaics. His methods of design were radically different from those taught in schools, earning him the admiration of some but bringing on the disdain of many of his colleagues. You can learn about his unusual techniques in the Gaudí museum housed inside La Pedrera (*see p51*) in Barcelona.

Inspired architecture of Parc Güell

Gaudí's Sagrada Familia

Gaudí's principal patron was the wealthy Catalan textile magnate Eusebi Güell. Güell funded some of Gaudí's major works, like the Parc Güell and the Palau Güell, a sombre creation intended as a residence for Güell and his wife. His best-known work, however, is the Temple of the Sagrada Familia (Holy Family), a looming church begun in the late 19th century. When it will be finished is anyone's guess; the estimated date of completion is 2050.

Gaudí was a deeply religious man, and his works were heavy with symbolism and messages. Many people mistakenly call Gaudí's work playful, fanciful or worthy of a fairy tale, but through his innovative shapes and techniques he was trying to express the perfection of the nature God created.

Interest in Gaudí's work began to fade by the second decade of the 20th century, and the architect was left without commissions or patrons. When he was run over by a tram in 1926 local taxi drivers assumed he was a vagrant and refused to take him to the hospital. He died virtually alone days later.

After his death, Gaudí's work continued to be largely ignored for decades, and there was even talk about demolishing buildings like the Casa Milá (also known as La Pedrera). Luckily for architecture lovers, tourism came to the rescue. The rediscovery of Gaudí began in Japan, where the architect became wildly popular in the 1980s. Thousands of Japanese tourists descended on Catalonia in search of Gaudí's work, spawning a wave of architectural tourism and promoting efforts to restore buildings like the Casa Milá and the Casa Battló. These days, Gaudí's work is a central part of Catalonia's identity, and millions of tourists visit his creations each year.

There is even a movement to make him a saint. According to the Association for the Beatification of Antoni Gaudí, the architect's utter devotion to the Church should be an example to other Catholics. The Vatican has already ushered the architect through the first steps of the process, and researchers are busy looking for evidence of miracles, so Gaudí may well be on his way to sainthood.

Festivals and events

Catalonia's calendar is packed with special events and festivals, ranging from tame religious celebrations to wild, all-night affairs. Nearly all major festes *(fiestas in Spanish, festivals in English) are accompanied by the towering* castellers *(see pp76–7), the stately* gegants *(giants) and the funny* capsgrossos *(literally, fat heads) who wander among the crowd.*

The giants can be up to three metres (10ft) tall and are elegant, life-like portrayals of famous Catalans. Strong-backed supporters climb inside the huge puppets and carry them on their shoulders. The *gegants'* opposite, the *capsgrossos*, are big-headed, squat characters that run around playfully.

Another common element in *festes* is fire. Firecrackers, fireworks and torches seem to have a permanent presence in Catalan festivals. In summer, *correfocs* (fire runs) are an almost obligatory part of the fun. They consist of dragons and monsters carrying torches and firecrackers through the streets while the crowd dares to see how close it can get to the action without getting burnt. Catalonia's best festivals and events are:

Three Kings' Day (6 January) The arrival of the three kings from the Orient is a big celebration throughout Catalonia. In elaborate processions through Barcelona and other towns the kings throw sweets to the children and promise to bring them gifts later in the night.

Carnaval (mid-February) The week before Lent is celebrated with abandon in some areas of Catalonia, especially in Sitges, where the gay-friendly parade is famous. A week of parties, concerts and fireworks ends with a huge *rúa* (parade) featuring fantastically elaborate costumes and dance routines.

Setmana Santa (Easter week, March–April) Catalonia, for all its Catholic tradition, is not a very religious area, and most people celebrate Holy Week with a trip to the beach or the mountains. The official celebration includes a special Palm Sunday service (where all kids are given a palm branch by their godmothers) and processions throughout the week, one of the most spectacular of which takes place in Tarragona.

Sant Jordí (23 April) St George, Catalonia's patron saint, is honoured with this charming holiday, when men give roses to their sweethearts and loved ones, and women give them books in return. On this day Catalonia fills with colourful book and flower stalls; one of the best places to browse or shop is Las Ramblas in Barcelona.

Corpus Christi (early June) Beginning the Thursday before Corpus, fountains throughout Barcelona are decked out with flowers and topped with a dancing egg. The raw egg is kept in balance by the weight of its yolk, and it spins atop a stream of water. Also interesting are the flower carpets created in Sitges; on Sunday you can stroll the streets among carnation petals and grass clippings that have been formed into intricate designs.

Sant Joan (St John the Baptist, 23–24 June) The shortest night of the year is a non-stop fireworks display in towns all over the region. The traditional *coca de Sant Joan*, a sweet bread, is served with cava, and bonfires provide the light for parties that last all night.

Festes de La Mercè (24 September) Barcelona's patroness is celebrated with days of concerts, cultural events and street fairs.

Tots Sants (1 November) Catalans celebrate All Saints' Day by visiting their families (dead and alive) and eating roasted *castanyas* (chestnuts) and *panelletes*, which are delicious almond sweets made only at this time of year.

Gigantes at the Festes de la Mercè in Barcelona

Impressions

Whether you're looking for the bustle of vibrant cities, soothing lush green landscapes or the gentle breeze of the Mediterranean, you'll find it in this diverse region. There's no way to neatly sum up the land of Catalonia, as the look and feel of the place changes from town to town.

Central **Barcelona** (*see p30*), the stylish capital, is the most cosmopolitan city of Spain, with fabulous food, shopping and nightlife. This modern city is a beacon for design and anything trendy, but as soon as you step beyond its borders the scene changes. Chic boutiques and minimalist style are quickly replaced with historic walled towns, rolling green vineyards and majestic scenery.

Southern Catalonia (*see p78*) is a largely rural area with the historic city of Tarragona, which is surrounded by the busy coastal resorts of the Costa Daurada, as its focal point. The Delta de l'Ebre, a huge swathe of wild, natural coastline, marks the southernmost border, while the hilly Priorat wine region runs through the interior.

North of Barcelona lie **Girona** and **La Costa Brava** (*see p94*), one of Catalonia's most popular destinations because of its rocky, cliff-strewn coast. Beach resorts line the Mediterranean, while medieval inland towns offer culture and history. Girona, the provincial capital, has a well-preserved Jewish quarter and is a fascinating place to explore.

The flatter plains of **central Catalonia** (*see p116*) stretch across the region's belly. This area is home to staunchly Catalan towns like Vic, Berga and Solsona, all busy places that don't make it on to the agenda of most foreign tourists. This is the place to see the true face of Catalonia: farmers selling their vegetables at the local market, women chatting with each other from their balconies and children playing in the streets.

Running along the northwestern border, the **Pyrenean and Pre-Pyrenean regions** (*see p122*) of La Cerdanya, Alt Urgell and the Vall d'Aran offer cool, tree-filled landscapes and quiet towns perfect for basing an excursion or skiing holiday. Come here in summer to escape the heat and the coastal crowds.

When to go

Given its mild weather and abundance of sunshine, any time is a good time to visit Catalonia. Beach weather begins in late May and lasts through October. Beaches are most crowded in July and August, when finding a spot to lay your towel can be a challenge along the coast. This is an excellent time to head into the Pyrenees, where you'll find sunny skies, cooler temperatures and ideal hiking conditions. Autumn and spring are good times to visit cities like Barcelona and Tarragona. In winter, try out ski resorts like Baqueira-Beret in the Pyrenees' Vall d'Aran.

Getting around

The best way to explore Catalonia is by car, especially if you plan to search out the historic towns and beautiful landscapes of central Catalonia and the Pyrenees, where public transport options are limited. Drivers tend to be aggressive, and the best way to deal with them is to be intelligently aggressive yourself. Keep in mind that many major highways are toll roads, including the AP-7 that runs from the French border to southern Catalonia, and the C-32 which runs along the coast. For information about car rental companies, *see p182.*

If you'd rather leave your wheels at home, train travel is another good option. The extensive RENFE train lines connect most large towns and cities as well as tourist destinations like Montserrat and the Port Aventura theme park. From Barcelona you can reach Tarragona or Girona in under an hour and a half. Resort towns like Tossa de Mar, Sitges and Salou are all on the railway lines too. Full schedules are online at *www.renfe.es*

Bus travel is less common, but it's often the only way to reach small towns if you don't have your own wheels.

Away from the coast and cities, Catalonia is still tranquilly rural

A seafront restaurant in Sitges

A variety of private bus companies operate in Catalonia; to buy tickets you'll need to contact the individual companies directly. Tourist offices can often help with this; you can also get contact information on *p186*.

Manners and customs

You'll find that Catalans are an efficient, businesslike bunch with little time for overt pleasantries. That doesn't mean, however, that they're rude, and politeness is highly valued here. Being too loud or inappropriately dressed in public places will draw stern looks, so be considerate of those around you, and be sure to wear proper shoes and shirts at all times, especially when you're visiting churches or historic monuments. Shorts and bare arms are tolerated in churches, though women should cover their shoulders.

In general, Catalans are very tolerant of foreigners, though they don't have the gregarious nature of other Spaniards. Expect to be ignored most of the time; foreigners are nothing new in Catalonia and seem to no longer draw the interest of locals, except those who rely on tourism for their livelihood! They won't expect you to speak Catalan but they don't particularly like to hear Spanish spoken.

Greetings

When you enter a store or restaurant, a general greeting of *bon día* (good day) is called for. As you leave, call out *adeu* (goodbye) to anyone who may be listening. Greeting friends is less formal; a simple *hola* (hello) or *¿Qué tal?* is fine.

Queues

Catalan queues might seem like mayhem, but they follow a strict protocol. As you approach a line call out *El últim?* (The last in line?) then keep your eye on that person and follow behind him. When someone comes behind you asking for *el últim*, just raise your hand.

Restaurants

Restaurants throughout Spain have a different standard of service from those in other countries. Waiters are generally not chatty or particularly friendly, but they're not trying to be rude. You in turn can be equally short back. A simple *'Vull la…'* (I want…) is the correct way to order. Be sure to request the bill (*la compta*), as it's considered rude for the waiter to put it on your table if you haven't asked for it.

Tipping

Catalans, known for being penny pinchers, are not big tippers. Simply rounding up the taxi fare or restaurant bill is considered good form, but leaving more than a 10 per cent tip is unusual. In nice hotels, tip bell boys about €1 per bag. At spas or hair salons tips are generally not accepted.

What to wear

Summers in Catalonia are warm and sunny, so bring light, loose clothing, plenty of sunscreen, a swimsuit and a hat. Topless bathing is accepted on most Catalan beaches, so the style of your swimsuit is all up to you. You'll want comfortable walking shoes and a good-size day pack (with a secure closure) for toting your camera and personal belongings. A jacket for breezy evenings is always a good idea, especially on the coast or in the Pyrenees.

In winter, the temperature can drop to 10°C (50°F) or lower, getting colder as you move towards the mountains.

Impressions

Catalans love to dance the Sardana, their national dance

You'll need a warm jacket, gloves and scarf from December to February. In the spring and autumn bring layers and an umbrella.

Remember that Catalans are elegant dressers and, while not overly formal, place much importance on style and appearance. To fit in with the locals avoid wearing trainers, baggy tee-shirts or sportswear like sweat pants. Dark, solid colours are easy to travel with and usually make the transition from day to night well. In summer, try to avoid wearing your beach clothes unless you're on the beach; it immediately marks you as a tourist!

Business hours

In Catalonia as in the rest of Spain, nearly every business closes at lunch. Banks, post offices and many government bodies are open mornings only, usually from 8am until 2pm. Shops open around 10am, close at 1.30pm or 2pm, and reopen at 3.30pm. Closing time is around 8.30pm, though it may be earlier in small towns.

Restaurants and bars

Eating in Catalonia should be one of the highlights of your holiday. With an abundance of fresh fish, local fruits and vegetables, and a booming culinary culture, good eating here is easy.

Esmorzar (breakfast) here is quick and informal. Though you'll find touristy restaurants and hotels serving full English-style breakfasts, the norm for Catalans is to grab a quick *café amb llet* (coffee with milk) and a croissant or *torrada* (toasted bread) topped with cheese or *mermelada* (marmalade). Some people go out for breakfast as late as 10am.

Dinar (lunch) rarely begins before 2pm and is the biggest meal of the day. Most people order a *primer plat* (first course), *segon plat* (entrée), *postre* (dessert) and *café* (coffee). Your best bet is to find a restaurant that serves a *menú del día* (fixed-price menu), a full three-course meal that usually costs around €10, drink included.

Sopar (dinner) comes at 8.30pm or later. When Catalans eat at home dinner is usually simple, often no more than a *truita amb patatas* (Spanish omelette) or *sopa* (soup). When they eat out dinner tends to be a long, drawn-out event lasting late into the night. Though most kitchens close by midnight, it's not unusual for tables to stay full of friends enjoying drinks and conversation until 1am or later.

Safety

Catalonia is not a particularly dangerous place, but you do need to take precautions, especially in cities and touristy areas. Pickpocketing is common, although not often violent, so always keep your belongings close by and under control. Tricky thieves may use scams to put you off guard; beware of someone who tells you that you have something on your shirt and then volunteers to help you to wipe it off (as they clean out your wallet too) or of groups of young people who crowd around you with a map asking for directions that they can never seem to properly understand. Other scams include the mock football game (a group of boys will kick a football your way and when you join in the game they'll crowd around you to nick your wallet) and the 'got a light?' routine (when one person will distract you by having you light their cigarette while another picks your pocket). Of course the standard bag snatch is still a threat too.

You also need to be careful about valuables left in your car; always keep

The simple pleasures of café life

purses, cameras and other belongings out of sight. Thieves are brazen about breaking windows to steal what's inside. In your hotel or apartment be sure to keep all doors locked (patio included), with valuables in a safe if possible.

Women travellers

Macho Spain does not exist the way it once did (though catcalls are still common) and Catalonia is a relatively safe and comfortable place for women travelling alone. Take precautions when walking alone at night; stick to well-travelled and well-lit areas, and try to leave valuables back at your hotel. In bars, keep an eye on your drink and don't accept drinks from strangers (unless you've seen the barman make it) to make sure no one slips something into it.

Gay and lesbian travellers

Coastal Catalonia is a friendly place for gay and lesbian travellers, especially in tolerant Barcelona and in Bohemian resort towns like Sitges, whose gay nightlife scene is famed throughout Europe. In Barcelona, most gay bars and shops are concentrated around an area of town dubbed 'Gaixample', which fans out from the intersection of Carrer Muntaner and Carrer Consell de Cent. Interior Catalonia is decidedly more conservative, and gay couples can expect to stand out a little more. For more information check out *www.gayinspain.com*

Barcelona

Barcelona is the second largest city in Spain, the capital of Catalonia. It has a magic that's hard to define. A seaside city along the Mediterranean coast with nearly two millennia of history, Barcelona's charm is found in its effortless ability to combine its storied past with a modern energy that's downright youthful in its vibrancy. This is taken full advantage of by the huge numbers of tourists it entertains all year round.

With its proud, shady boulevards and lively old quarter, Barcelona is a city meant to be strolled through and soaked up slowly. Its soul is found out on its streets and squares, where terrace cafés provide the ideal place to watch Barcelona waltz by. Nowhere does the city show itself with as much colour as on Las Ramblas, a pedestrian boulevard lined with everything from street performers to hamster vendors and fragrant flower stalls.

Thanks to its thriving arts scene and outstanding Modernist architecture,

Barcelona is full of interesting streets and squares

Sculpture in the Plaça de Catalunya

Barcelona is also one of Europe's great cultural centres. Gaudí, Picasso and Dalí all called this Mediterranean city home at one time or another, leaving a creative legacy that still haunts the galleries and young artists' workshops of today. More than half the city's museums are dedicated to modern art in one form or another, proving the city's fascination with everything new and innovative.

At night, the city's bars, terraces and clubs come alive, making Barcelona a great destination for nightlife. *Barris* (neighbourhoods) like La Ribera and Gràcia are packed with intimate spots where you can sit back with a glass of local *tinto* (red wine) or a *clara* (shandy) and watch the world go by. By night there are concerts at venues throughout the city, open-air performances in summer, and *discotecas* that will keep you dancing till dawn.

Barcelona loves to party, and the year is full of fiestas and festivals (*see pp22–3*). The biggest party of the year is La Mercè, the week-long party in honour of the city's patroness. Other must-see events are the guitar festival in spring, the El Greco cultural festival in June and July and the kid-friendly Three Kings' Day in January.

Barcelona's modern architecture

Barcelona has been at the cutting edge of Spanish architecture ever since the Modernists began work in the late 1800s, and the city proves as worthy as ever of its reputation as a design and architectural centre. Barcelona's style today is clean-lined, functional and innovative. Though Franco's dictatorship put a lid on designers' creativity through the 1950s, 60s and 70s, when ugly brick eyesores were the only things being built, by the 1980s Barcelona had come back into its own. The city made a concerted effort to reclaim its historic heritage and to create the buildings that would make tomorrow's history, using the 1992 Olympic Games as the excuse to spend millions overhauling huge swathes of the city.

In preparation for the Games, the city transformed its waterfront with a new port and spruced up the mountain of Montjuïc, the so-called 'Central Park' of Barcelona. A huge stadium was built, a maritime boulevard was constructed, and

The new suburb of Diagonal Mar

The futuristic Forum building

apartments were put up along the waterfront, completely changing entire Barcelona *barris*.

Those efforts served to put Barcelona on the map as a must-visit destination, but since then Barcelona has continued to build and reform, pushed by a string of civic-minded socialist mayors eager to boost Barcelona's reputation in the eyes of the world. Now the focus is on Barcelona's northern coast, where a new *barri* dubbed 'Diagonal Mar' has been created where there was once only a marginalised area full of smoky factories and crime. In 2004 Barcelona opened the ultra-modern Forum building (a creation that's been optimistically called the 'Guggenheim of Barcelona'), site of that year's Forum of Cultures festival. The blue, triangular building was designed by

Swiss architects Herzog and De Meuron and sits slightly suspended on mammoth columns. Southern Europe's largest conference centre was also built on the site, as was a new port, beach and park. In response, a host of sleek new offices, apartments and hotels now fills the district.

Another notable on Barcelona's building list is the Torre Agbar, an openly phallic skyscraper by French architect Jean Nouvel. Completed in 2004, this bullet-shaped tower has been compared to everything from a cigar to a tampon. The futuristic design sits in the centre of the busy Plaça de les Glòries Catalanas and is visible from all over Barcelona. At first residents were uncomfortable with the idea that this odd-shaped creation was destined to become a symbol of the city, but ever eager to be at the cutting edge the city has adapted to it, claiming the tower as one more proof of Barcelona's creativity.

Also keep an eye out for the old Las Arenas bullring, near Plaça Espanya, which is being turned into a shopping and entertainment centre. Famed architect Richard Rogers has teamed up with a local company to gut the inside of the old bullring and create a dynamic space where old Spanish culture and new bargain buys meet.

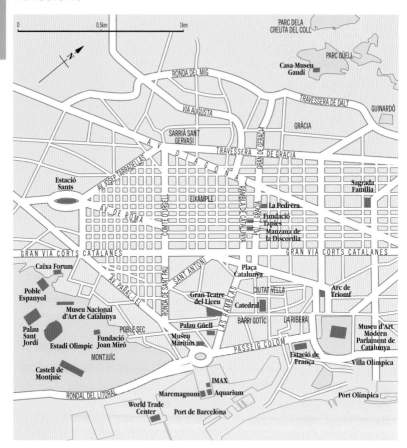

Orientation

Hemmed in by the Mediterranean and low mountains on three sides, Barcelona sits inside a sort of bowl that spills into the sea. The most interesting sights for the traveller are in the lower part of the city, in the Ciutat Vella, along Las Ramblas and on the stylish boulevards of the Eixample district.

The heart of Barcelona is the Plaça Catalunya, a sprawling square that links the Ciutat Vella (Old City) with the modern city. Running off the plaza is Las Ramblas, a bustling pedestrian boulevard that zips down to the Mediterranean coast and the city's ports. As you walk down Las Ramblas, El Raval, a former red-light district that has morphed into a creative hotspot, is on your right and the Barri Gòtic (Gothic Quarter) stretches out to the left. Beyond the Barri Gòtic is the medieval *barri* of La Ribera, home to the Picasso Museum and the beautiful Santa María del Mar Basilica.

North of Plaça Catalunya is the sprawling neighbourhood known as L'Eixample (The Extension). Built in the late 19th century, it boasts an easy-to-navigate grid layout and most of the city's Modernist buildings. The neighbourhood's major boulevards are Passeig de Gràcia, which runs like an arrow through L'Eixample, dividing it into two neat east and west districts, and El Diagonal, which crosses all of Barcelona and marks L'Eixample's upper boundary.

Beyond El Diagonal are the *barris* of Gràcia, an artsy district, and Sarrià, the city's upmarket neighbourhood. If you keep heading up the hill you'll come to the mountain of Tibidabo, where a funfair is open in summer, and the Collserola ridge, full of walking paths.

Barri Gòtic

A maze of narrow cobblestone streets where tiny plazas seem to materialise out of nothing and history pops out at every turn, Barcelona's Barri Gòtic (Gothic Quarter) is one of its most magical neighbourhoods. Yes, this area is home to the cathedral and a few

Cathedral, Barri Gòtic

View of Barcelona from Tibidabo mountain

Ciutat Vella (Old Town)

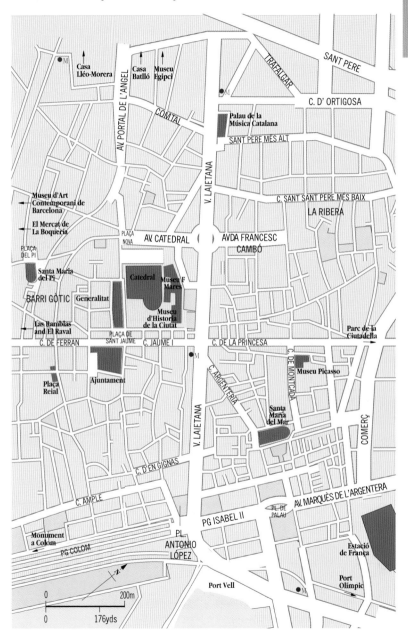

other Gothic monuments, but the Barri Gòtic also hides Romanesque palaces, Roman ruins and Renaissance houses. The best way to experience this historic district is to lose yourself in the sights, sounds and smells of its winding streets (see the Barri Gòtic Walk on *pp42–3*) but there are a few specific sights worth seeking out.

Museu d'Història de la Ciutat de Barcelona (Barcelona City History Museum)

Hidden underneath the pretty Plaça del Rei are stones that tell the story of Barcelona's first years as a city. Low Roman ruins reveal the outlines of an ancient winery, a few homes, streets complete with gutters, a textile factory and a sauce-making factory.

Plaça del Rei. Tel: 93 315 1111; www.museuhistoria.bcn.es. Open: Tue–Sat 10am–2pm & 4–8pm (June–Sept 10am–8pm), Sun 10am–2pm. Admission charge. Metro: Jaume I.

Museu Diocesà de Barcelona

Nestling in the city's ancient Roman wall, this small museum has an exceptional collection of sacred art, including pieces like the silver monstrance of the Church of Santa María del Pi and contemporary art.

Plaça del Rei – 'the square of the king' – is full of fantastic architecture

*Avinguda de la Catedral 4.
Tel: 93 315 2213. Open: Tue–Sat
10am–2pm & 5–8pm, Sun 11am–2pm.
Admission charge. Metro: Jaume I.*

Plaça Sant Jaume

This sunny, open square is the site for
the never-ending face-off between the
Generalitat (the seat of Catalan
government) and the Ajuntament
(Town Hall). The medieval Palau de la
Generalitat features a pretty orange
grove that's decorated in Catalan
colours on Catalan holidays. The
Ajuntament was built piecemeal from
the 14th to the 19th century, and the
elegant Saló de Cent (Chamber of 100),
built 1373, is its best feature.

*Plaça Sant Jaume. Generalitat.
Tel: 93 402 4617. Tours given second and
fourth Sun 10.30am–1.30pm.
Ajuntament. Plaça Sant Jaume.
Tel: 93 402 7000. Open for visits Sun
10am–1.30pm. Metro: Jaume I.*

Plaça del Pi

This shady square, home to occasional
open-air markets and plenty of
pavement cafés, is one of the *barri*'s
most emblematic spots. It's dominated
by the Catalan Gothic Església de Santa
María del Pi, an imposing 14th-century
church. With its harsh, unadorned
façade and calm interior air, this church
is generally considered Barcelona's
second-best example of Catalan Gothic,
the first being Santa María del Mar
(*see p46*). The plaza here was once the
church cemetery.

Medieval window in the Barri Gòtic

*Plaça del Pi. Church open:
8.30am–1.30pm & 3–4.30pm, Sun
9am–2pm & 5–9pm. Metro: Liceu.*

Catedral de Santa Eulàlia

The splendid Gothic creation standing
here today was built in the 14th
century, but this site has been a
continuous place of worship ever since
the first modest Christian chapel was
built here more than 1,500 years ago.

SANTA EULÀLIA

While walking on the Baixada de Santa
Eulàlia, pause a moment to remember the
martyred 13-year-old saint, one of Barcelona's
two patronesses. According to legend, she was
put in a barrel full of knives and rolled down
this street to her death for refusing the
romantic advances of a non-Christian soldier.

The cathedral's façade was added in the 19th century

Barcelona's cathedral is best seen from the outside, glittering with ornate detail beside the busy Plaça de la Seu. By day its spires stand out brilliantly against the deep blue sky, while by night it's softly lit, giving the plaza in front an unbeatably romantic air. Inside, the cathedral can be a bit dark and gloomy. Yet what it lacks in ambience it makes up for in sheer glorious size; this is a massive church, designed to make you feel small and the heavens to seem weighty.

History
Soon after Christianity became the official religion of the Roman Empire, a small basilica was built on this site. It remained the city's main place of worship for centuries but was destroyed in 925 when Muslim forces stormed the city. A century later, a Romanesque cathedral was built on the same spot. You can still see vestiges of that early house of worship in the Capella de Santa Lucía, a pretty chapel that was incorporated into the main cathedral. The cathedral you see today was begun in 1298 and was not declared complete until 1870, when the neo-Gothic façade was tacked on thanks to the philanthropic efforts of wealthy Catalan banker Manuel Girona.

The interior
The cathedral boasts three large naves lined with chapels and endless examples of excellent Gothic artwork. Seek out the statue of Sant Crist de Lepant (Christ of Lepanto), in the chapel of the same name. Legend says that the statue was carried into the Battle of Lepanto (1571) and was able to bend its body into an 'S' shape to avoid being smashed by a cannonball. The chapel itself is a lovely example of pure Gothic construction; crane your neck to marvel at the vaulted roof. The 14th-century choir stalls, the small cathedral museum and the crypt, accessible by stairs near the main altar, are also worth checking out. For views of the Barri Gòtic, take the lift up to the roof.

The façade
It's hard to believe that the cathedral's elaborate façade was added on more

built between 1382 and 1448, it has a lush garden surrounded by delicate arcades. Inside, 13 white geese waddle about; supposedly they symbolise the purity of the virgin St Eulàlia (*see p39*), who is buried in the cathedral's crypt.

Come by the cloister during Corpus Christi (*see p23*), when the fountain here is decked out with flowers and the famous *l'ou com balla* (the dancing egg) is set atop the fountain's stream of water to twirl and 'dance' away.

Cathedral, Pla de la Seu. Tel: 93 402 8260. Open: Mon–Sat 1.15–4.30pm, Sun 2–5.15pm. Free admission but donation suggested. Metro: Jaume 1.

The massive pillars and high vaults of Santa Eulàlia

than 400 years after the rest of the structure was deemed complete. Though based on a 1408 design, the front façade's style contrasts sharply with other exterior details. If you walk around the back of the cathedral you'll see the straight lines and plain walls of traditional Catalan Gothic, adorned only by a few feebly ferocious gargoyles. Some of them are outright comical: the ones on the southeastern wall, near the Plaça del Rei, depict awkward renditions of exotic animals like elephants and unicorns, obviously creatures the sculptor had never seen.

The cloister

This is most people's favourite part of the cathedral. A quiet, breezy enclosure

White geese are kept in the cloister

Walk: Barri Gòtic

This walk takes you through the oldest part of the city, past Roman walls, Romanesque chapels and Gothic monuments. Much of what you see has been faithfully restored and goes a long way in revealing the city's history.

While you could easily spend days wandering the narrow stone streets of the barri, *this itinerary will take you through the Gothic quarter in about an hour, plus the time you spend inside the monuments.*

1 Plaça Nova

Begin the walk at the so-called 'New Square', which is right by the cathedral and was cleared in 1355. This was one of the main city gates, and you can still see part of the old Roman wall on your left as you head down Carrer Bisbe.

2 The Turtle

Take a quick detour down the first street on your left (Carrer de Santa Llúcia) to eye the odd decoration on the City Archives building. The mail box is adorned with an image of a turtle: could the artist have been mocking Spain's notoriously slow mail service?

3 Plaça de Sant Felip Neri

As you walk up Carrer Bisbe, take your first right at the Plaça de Garriga i Bachs and make your way down the narrow alley here to find the quiet Plaça de Sant

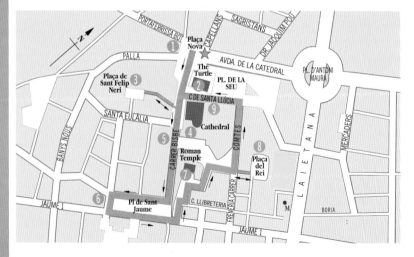

Felip Neri, a quiet oasis amid the buzz of the city. Take note of the coppersmiths' and shoemakers' guild houses (which were moved here in the 1950s to make way for the new Avinguda de la Catedral); both have markings of their guild, tools and shoes, on the façades. The church shows traces of bomb damage which killed 20 children, a chilling reminder of the cruelty of Spain's Civil War.

Neo-Gothic bridge on Carrer Bisbe

4 Cathedral cloister

Back on Carrer Bisbe, take a moment to duck into the cathedral's cloister on your left. The geese filling the grassy interior courtyard get most of the attention, but also pay attention to the gravestones embedded in the floor; many bear symbols that give clues to who is buried there. For example, an etching of scissors suggests that a tailor is buried there, while that of a shoe suggests the grave of a shoemaker.

5 Carrer Bisbe

Just past the cloister entrance is a neo-Gothic bridge spanning the narrow street. This lovely piece of art is one of the most often photographed sights in Barcelona, but it's not an original part of the *barri* at all: it was added in the 1920s by the architect Joan Rubió i Bellvé.

6 Plaça de Sant Jaume

At the end of Carrer Bisbe you'll find yourself in the wide open Plaça de Sant Jaume, home to the Ajuntament and Generalitat.

7 Roman temple

Turn back towards Carrer Bisbe but take a right on to Carrer Llibreteria and then a quick left on to Carrer Paradís. At number 10 on your left is the Centre Excursionista de Catalunya, inside which you'll find all that remains of a 1st-century Roman temple.
Centre Excursionista de Catalunya. Tel: 93 319 0222. Open Tue–Sun 10am–2pm & 4–8pm.

8 Plaça del Rei

The Carrer Paradís enters a small plaza just behind the cathedral. Turn right and cross the entire plaza. You'll soon come to another open space, the Plaça del Rei, a charming medieval square beside the Royal Palace. Concerts are often held here in summer.

9 Cathedral

Head up to Carrer Comtes to end up at the cathedral entrance and the end of the walk.

Las Ramblas is famed for its flower stalls

Las Ramblas and El Raval

Las Ramblas is perhaps Spain's most famous street, with a boisterous atmosphere day and night and enough street performers and artists to keep you freely entertained for days. Just off Las Ramblas is El Raval, a working-class neighbourhood that's one of the city's most diverse. Though once the red-light district, El Raval has cleaned itself up in recent years and is now known for its quirky bars and creative shops.

Las Ramblas

The word *rambla* means stream or creek, and this long pedestrian thoroughfare is so named because it was built atop a filled-in creek. The street came into being slowly as the Cagallel creek was clogged up and filled in bit by bit. By the mid-18th-century it was appearing on maps, and by later in the century it was a proper avenue. Las Ramblas goes through many name changes as it runs its course from the Plaça de Catalunya to the sea.

El Gran Teatre del Liceu

Barcelona's fabulously ornate opera house, the Liceu was first inaugurated in 1847 and has always been a city landmark. It was reopened in 1999 after a serious fire destroyed the lush interior. In the guided tour you can see the 'Hall of Mirrors', the posh foyer and the concert hall.
Las Ramblas 61–65. Tel: 93 485 9914; www.liceubarcelona.com. Open: visits at 10am, 11.30am, 12pm, 1pm. Admission charge. Metro: Liceu

El Mercat de La Boquería

For the uninitiated, a stroll around this emblematic fresh market, with its stalls hawking live crabs, beef tripe and ox tails, can be a startling experience, but it makes for a great photo opportunity.
Las Ramblas 91. Tel: 93 318 2584. Open: Mon–Sat 8am–8.30pm. Metro: Liceu.

Monument a Colom

Zip up the elevator to the top of this statue of Christopher Columbus for a panoramic view of the port and lower Barcelona.
Plaça Portal de la Pau. Tel: 93 302 5224. Open: Oct–May Mon–Sun 10am–6.30pm; June–Sept 9am–8.30pm. Admission charge. Metro: Drassanes.

Museu d'Art Contemporani de Barcelona (Museum of Contemporary Art – MACBA)

Designed by American architect Richard Meier and opened in 1995, the gleaming white exterior of the MACBA offers nearly as good a show as the contemporary artwork within its walls. Ever-changing exhibits feature Spanish and international works from the past 50 years.

Plaça dels Àngels 1. Tel: 93 412 0810; www.macba.es. Open: Mon–Fri 11am–7.30pm, Sat 10am–8pm, Sun 10am–3pm. Admission charge. Metro: Catalunya and Universitat.

Museu Marítim

Sitting in what once were the royal shipyards, this is a surprisingly interesting museum that looks at Catalonia's seafaring history.

Avinguda Drassanes. Tel: 93 342 9920; www.museummaritimbarcelona.org. Open: daily 10am–7pm. Admission charge, free first Sat afternoon of month. Metro: Drassanes.

Plaça Reial

A pretty arcaded square, the 'Royal Plaza' was built in the 19th century in a neoclassical style. These days it's filled with restaurants and terrace cafés. Getting a coffee or an evening beer here is an atmospheric but pricey experience, though it's probably worth doing at least once. This area is known for being a hangout for drug dealers and their clients, so do be careful with your belongings.

The Plaça Reial is picturesque and lively

Sant Pere and La Ribera

This charming *barri* was a bustling centre of trade in medieval Barcelona, and you can see remnants of those days in the street names like Carrer de l'Argenteria (Silversmith's Street), Carrer de la Vidrieria (Glassblower's Street) and Carrer de Corders (Ropemaker's Street). Modern Ribera is known as a centre of art and design, with loads of fashionable shops, bars and restaurants that make it one of the city's best areas for exploring day or night.

Basílica de Santa María del Mar

Generally considered the best example of Catalan Gothic architecture, this

Santa María del Mar, Catalan Gothic at its purest

WINE BAR TOUR

La Ribera is home to some of Barcelona's best wine bars, and a wine bar 'crawl' is a great way to spend an evening here. Start the route at La Vinya del Senyor (*Plaça Santa María 5*), an intimate bar whose outdoor tables hide under the shadow of the Basilica. Next head to stylish Va de Vi (*Carrer Banys Vells 16*), a chic bar housed in a medieval house that still has its original doorway and walls. End the crawl with a glass of bubbly at El Xampanyet (*Carrer Montcada 22*), a *barri* favourite that's been serving local cava for generations.

If you want to buy a few bottles for the road, stop by the wine superstore Vila Viniteca (*Carrer Agullers 7*), a neighbourhood institution, or at the sleek new shop La Carte des Vins (*Carrer Sombrers 1*), where the manager is a former chef who can advise about how to pair wine and food.

elegant basilica was built in the mid-1300s by and for the people of the *barri*. Its interior was gutted in anti-Church riots in the 20th century, so pretty much all we see today are the lovely bones of the structure itself. *Plaça de Santa María del Mar. Tel: 93 310 2390. Open: Mon–Sat 9am–1.30pm & 4.30–8pm, Sun opens 10am. Metro: Jaume I.*

Museu Picasso

With works spanning the Málaga-born artist's entire career and an emphasis on the works of his early years, this museum is a must for Picasso lovers. Picasso lived in Barcelona from 1895 to 1904 and had his first exhibition in Els Quatre Gats, a tavern in the city (*see p53*), so Barcelona claims him as an adopted son. The museum, renovated

in 2003, fills the interiors of five connecting medieval palaces.
Carrer Montcada 15–23. Tel: 93 319 6310; www.museupicasso.bcn.es. Open: Tue–Sun 10am–8pm. Admission charge, free 1st Sun of the month. Metro: Jaume 1.

Palau de la Música Catalana

A masterpiece of Modernism designed by Lluis Domènech i Montaner in 1905, the Palace of Catalan Music is a symphony for the eyes, with coloured glass, mosaics and sculptures over every surface. The tours here are fascinating, but to get the essence of the Palau attend a concert inside.
Carrer Sant Francesc de Paula 2. Tel: 93 295 7200; www.palaumusica.org. Open: 10am–3.30pm; Aug 10am–6pm. Admission charge. Metro: Urquinaona.

Ports and shore

For centuries, Barcelona lived with 'her back turned to the sea'. The waterfront was the domain of poor fishermen, and one of the few things built with a view of the Mediterranean was the city's cemetery on the slope of Montjuïc. All that changed with the 1992 Olympics, when Barcelona reclaimed the waterfront and established a brand-new port and sandy beaches.

Parc de la Ciutadella

When the hated Ciutadella fortress was razed in the 18th century, this lush park was later set up on the site. Originally built for the 1888 World Expo, the park has a fine layout, with big grassy fields for lounging, wide paths for strolling and a pretty pond crowned with an elaborate monument. You can rent

The Palau de la Música Catalana is a UNESCO World Heritage Site

Floating restaurants and moored yachts line Port Vell

rowing boats here. Also in the park is Barcelona's small but well-kept zoo. Sadly, the zoo's most famous resident, a unique albino gorilla named Snowflake, died of skin cancer in 2004.

Parc de la Ciutadella. Passeig Picasso. Open: Apr–Sept daily 8am–10pm, Oct–Mar 8am–8pm. Zoo. Parc de la Ciutadella. Tel: 93 225 6787; www.zoobarcelona.com. Open 9.30am–7.30pm in summer, 10am–5pm in winter. Admission charge. Metro: Arc de Triumf.

Port Vell

Barcelona's 'Old Port' is surrounded by posh yachts and restaurants offering delicious seafood creations. At its centre is Maremàgnum, an entertainment complex with shops, restaurants, dance clubs and a mini-golf course on the roof. The most charming aspect of the port is the 'Rambla del Mar', a wooden footbridge that acts like a waterside extension of Las Ramblas.

Metro: Drassanes.

Port Olímpic

Built for the Olympics in 1992, the Olympic port is packed with restaurants and nightlife options. Come here for paella and pop music that lasts late into the night all week long.
Metro: Vila Olímpic.

Forum site

In the summer of 2004 Barcelona hosted a mammoth cultural festival called the Forum of Cultures, and it was held at this sprawling site. The park, beach and port here were all purpose-built for the occasion, as was the startlingly modern Forum building itself (*see p33*).
Metro: Maresme Forum (line 4).

OUTDOOR MUSEUM

Creations by top artists dot the area around Barcelona's waterfront, making this a virtual outdoor museum of contemporary art. Keep an eye out for Barcelona Head, a colourful work by Roy Lichtenstein that sits at the base of Via Laietana, Frank Gehry's Fish, which dominates the waterfront of the new Olympic Port, and Rebecca Horn's Wounded Star, a tower in homage to Barceloneta.

L'Eixample

By the 1800s, medieval Barcelona had grown way too cramped for comfort, and the city sought out ways to expand. In 1859 a utopian design by engineer Ildefons Cerdà was chosen to be the new Barcelona, and the grid-like Eixample district was born. Cerdà

Barcelona

The Rambla del Mar

imagined wide boulevards and apartments built around small gardens; the reality is somewhat different, as a short stroll will show. Still, this orderly neighbourhood is a far cry from the narrow alleys of the Barri Gòtic. The new *barri* became a blank slate for the Modernist architects to create upon.

Modern-day L'Eixample is a stylish place loaded with shopping options and restaurants. Much of Barcelona's population lives and works here, so it's a very active quarter that will give you insight into 'real' Barcelona life.

Fundació Antoni Tàpies

Housed in a striking Modernist building designed by Domènech i Montaner, the Tàpies Foundation houses the world's most comprehensive collection of works by this prolific Catalan artist. The surprising mass of metal and wire on top of the building is Cloud and Chair, an original work by Tàpies and a taste of what's to come inside. Cultural events are held here regularly.
Carrer Aragó 255. Tel: 93 487 0315. Open: Tue–Sun 10am–8pm. Admission charge. Metro: Passeig de Gràcia.

La Manzana de la Discordia and Casa Batlló

This city block on Passeig de Gràcia is proof of the not-so-subtle rivalry between architectural contemporaries Gaudí, Domènech i Montaner and Puig i Cadafalch. Each built a splendid house on this one city block, and they

The 'Block of Discord'

obviously didn't consult one another about styles or colours, and the utterly different styles led the Barcelonese to dub this the La Manzana de la Discordia, the 'Block of Discord'. The name is a pun, *manzana* meaning both 'city block' and 'apple' – so the name can be taken as 'Apple of Discord', referring to the Greek myth of the Judgement of Paris.

Without doubt, the best of the three is the Casa Batlló, an allegorical design that tells the story of St George and the dragon (*see p16*).
Manzana de la Discordia. Passeig de Gràcia 35–45 (between Carrer Consell de Cent and Carrer d'Aragò. Metro: Passeig de Gràcia.
Casa Battló. Passeig de Gràcia 43.

Tel: 93 216 0306; www.casabattlo.es.
Open: 9am–8pm. Admission charge.
Metro: Passeig de Gràcia.

La Pedrera

Officially called the Casa Milà, this is one of Antoni Gaudí's best-known works. Not your standard apartment complex, it is classic Gaudí, with a curving, granite façade that has been compared to the waves of the Mediterranean and to the peaks of Montserrat. Inside, the architect supposedly used no straight lines in its basic construction. If he did, they are hard to spot amid the twisted balconies, swirling staircases and fanciful décor.

Though people still live in parts of the building, one section has been turned into the Espai Gaudí, a museum of Gaudí's work. This is an excellent place for the first-timer to get a handle on the architect's style and technique. Be sure to head up to the rooftop to ramble among the oddly shaped chimneys. In summer, concerts are held here weekend nights, but you have to order tickets several days in advance. *Passeig de Gràcia 92. Tel: 90 240 0973. Open: 10am–8pm. Admission charge. Metro: Diagonal.*

Museu Egipci

Run by a local hotel owner, this fascinating museum showcases more than 700 Egyptian artefacts and is a fascinating look at this ancient culture. *Carrer València 284. Tel: 93 488 0188; www.fundclos.com. Open: Mon–Sat 10am–8pm, Sun 10am–2pm. Admission charge. Metro: Passeig de Gràcia.*

A busy boulevard in L'Eixample

Modernisme

Balconies of Montaner's Casa Lleó – Morera

Modernisme is the Catalan variant of the Art Nouveau movement that struck Europe in the early 20th century, and it struck particularly hard in bourgeois Barcelona. Don't be deceived by the word itself. Catalan Modernism has nothing to do with what English speakers call Modernist art, which covers just about any painting or sculpture done in the 20th century. True Modernisme refers only to the brief window between 1890 and 1910.

By 1900 Modernisme was a commonly known style, an almost overused word used to describe those artists, writers, architects and designers who sought to break with austere traditions of the past and incorporate art into their everyday lives. They were inspired by nature and by everyday people doing everyday things. They believed that art was more than what's on a canvas, that it could be the things that surround us all the time. So furniture, jewellery, pottery, metalwork and even textiles were used as mediums of expression. You can still see the evidence of this attitude if you pay attention to details on buildings or in pharmacies as you stroll through L'Eixample. Elaborate doorways are surrounded by sculptures, while interiors often boast intricate chandeliers or elegant furniture.

Common subjects were flowers, birds, insects and sensuous women,

Detail from Parc Güell

all usually portrayed with smooth, curving lines and vivid colours. Nationalist Catalan symbols, like the dragon and bat, also appeared frequently in Modernist works, and Catalan Modernisme was linked closely to the Renaixança (Catalan Renaissance), a popular effort to reclaim the glories of Catalonia's past. Nearly all Modernist artists were marked by a seemingly contradictory tendency to look backwards and forwards at the same time, struggling to drag Catalan culture out of oblivion and push it towards new heights. Architects showed the influence of the past in their use of Catalan symbols and also in their assimilation of techniques originally used in Catalan Gothic or *mudéjar* (Moorish-Spanish) styles, while at the same time they shocked their contemporaries with innovative building styles and methods.

Reus native Antoni Gaudí was Modernisme's best-known proponent, but he was far from the only one. Other excellent architects, among them Lluís Doménech i Montaner and Josep Puig i Cadafalch, contributed in huge ways to Modernisme, leaving Barcelona's L'Eixample strewn with their works.

Artists like Ramón Casas and Santiago Rusiñol worked on canvas instead of on city blocks. Like the architects, they earned their keep working for the members of Barcelona's large and extravagant upper class, many of whom owed their wealth to the booming trade between Spain and Cuba. Casas and Rusiñol never earned much fame beyond Catalonia, but here they were and are highly regarded for their thoughtful paintings depicting everyday life in Catalonia. They're perhaps most known for founding the Quatre Gats tavern. Today a stylish café and restaurant, Els Quatre Gats (*Carrer de Montsió 3. Tel: 93 302 4140*) was originally a meeting place for bohemian artists and thinkers. Pablo Picasso held his first exhibition here and other artists of the day came here to talk and drink.

Gaudí's Casa Battló

La Sagrada Familia

The Templo de la Sagrada Familia (Temple of the Holy Family) is Barcelona's most famous sight. It is Antoni Gaudí's unfinished masterpiece, an awe-inspiring creation loaded with symbolism and intricate detailing.

History

Construction on the Sagrada Familia began in 1882, but when Gaudí was put on the project a year later he started nearly from scratch, laying out a new plan that featured five naves in the main church and a glorious dome 170m (558ft) tall. Gaudí was a devout Catholic, and he worked on the church for the rest of his life, accepting no

The towering façade of Sagrada Familia

payment for his services. For years he even lived in the church's crypt, dedicating himself body and soul to its creation. Because of economic difficulties construction moved forward in fits and starts, and during his lifetime the architect would see the completion of only a façade and a single belltower.

Gaudí was run over by a tram and died in 1926, so work carried on under the direction of his assistants, who followed the plans and models he had left. When these were destroyed in a fire in 1936 during the Civil War, Gaudí's original visions were largely lost. In 1940, architect Fransesc Quintana tried to recover some of what was damaged in the fire, and he restored some of the old models in an effort to piece

The light and airy nave

together Gaudí's vision. The work that carries on today is largely based on those models.

Work has continued under various different architects from that time until now. Today we can see eight of the planned twelve towers (which represent the twelve apostles) and the vaults of the main nave. The church is striking as it is; it's hard to imagine what effect it will give when one day the twelve towers rise majestically around the mammoth central dome.

Nativity façade

Built by Gaudí himself, this face includes four towers decorated with elaborate mosaics. You can climb two of the towers to see the mosaics up close and get a great view of Barcelona. It gets its name from the theme represented in the portal: the manger surrounded by animals and angels.

Passion façade

Representing Jesus' last days, this façade is full of sombre sculptures created from the 1950s onward. Most work was directed by famed Catalan artist Josep Subirachs, whose style is markedly different from Gaudí's. There's a lift that will take you to the top of one of the four towers for a different perspective.

Interior

Right now the church's main nave is a construction site, with workers cutting stone, modelling plaster and

hammering most of the day. When finished, the interior will be laden with decoration and symbols. For now enjoy the organic forms of the support pillars (they look like trees with branches to support the roof) and the windows (blooming flowers that will one day be filled with coloured glass).
Carrer Mallorca 401. Tel: 93 207 3031; www.sagradafamilia.org. Open: Oct–Mar 9am–6pm, Apr–Sept 9am–8pm. Admission charge. Metro: Sagrada Familia.

La Sagrada Familia's iconic spires

Walk: Modernisme

The majority of Barcelona's Modernist works are scattered about L'Eixample, but traces of the style can be seen all over Barcelona. This route takes you from the heart of the old city up through L'Eixample, ending at La Sagrada Familia.

Plan at least two hours, much more if you plan to stop for visits.

1 Palau Güell

Start your walk on Carrer Nou de la Rambla no 3. at the Palau Güell, designed by Antoni Gaudí in 1886. It's a rather austere house that was built for Gaudí's patron Eusebi Güell. Pay attention to the exquisite ironwork on the façade; it's considered some of the best of its kind in Barcelona.

Carrer Nou de la Rambla 3. Tel: 93 317 3974; www.bcn.es. Open: Mon–Sat 10am–1.45pm. Admission charge.

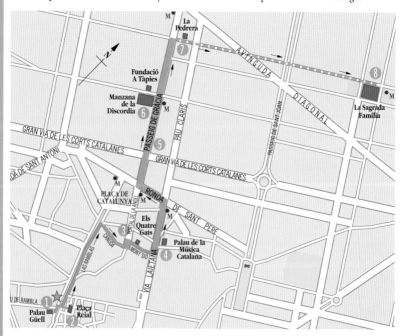

2 Plaça Reial

Head up Las Ramblas and pause to take a peek in the Plaça Reial, where lampposts designed by a young Gaudí in 1878 dot the square.

3 Els Quatre Gats

Back on Las Ramblas head up a few more blocks and turn right on Carrer de la Canuda. Take your third left on to Portal de l'Angel and then your first right on to Carrer de Montsió to stop in Els Quatre Gats (no 3, *see p53*), designed by Josep Puig i Cadafalch.

4 Palau de la Música Catalana

Back on the street, continue east until you reach the busy Via Laietana. Turn left and then take the second right on to Carrer Sant Pere Més Alt. Here you'll find the Palau de la Música Catalana in all its splendour.

5 Passeig de Gràcia

Make a beeline up Via Laietana to the Plaça Urquinaona. From here walk left on the Ronda de Sant Pere to reach the Passeig de Gràcia, the best Modernist canvas in the city.

6 La Manzana de la Discordia

The left side of Carrer Consell de Cent is the Manzana de la Discordia (Block of Discord). The first house you come to is the Casa Lleó Morera (no 35), Domènech i Montaner's 1902 design that uses floral motifs throughout. Next door is Puig i Cadafalch's Casa Amatller, built in 1898 for a man who

The intricate façade of the Palau Güell

earned his wealth in the chocolate industry. Notice the *mudéjar* elements on the façade. Now the this building houses the Centro de Modernisme, where you can get information about Modernist routes and tours. At the end of the block, Gaudí's glittering Casa Batlló is by far the most interesting of the three.

7 La Pedrera

Keep walking up Passeig de Gràcia and soon the undulating façade of the Casa Milà (otherwise known as La Pedrera) appears on your right.

8 Sagrada Familia

From here the Sagrada Familia Church is about ten city blocks away. Walk or get there more quickly on the Metro. Line 5 stops at the intersection of Diagonal/Passeig de Gràcia and at La Sagrada Familia.

Gràcia and beyond

Not all of Barcelona's charms are in its centre. Head to Gràcia for quirky shops and chill nights out, to Camp Nou for a look into one of Spain's top football clubs, or to Tibidabo for great city views and a charming old-time funfair.

Camp Nou

Fans of Barça (Fútbol Club Barcelona) will want to check out the extensive museum dedicated to the club and its history. You'll also get a guided tour of the massive stadium itself, which can seat 100,000 fans.
Carrer Arístides Maillol gates 7 & 9. Tel: 93 496 3608; www.fcbarcelona.com. Open: Mon–Sat 10am–6.30pm, Sun 10am–2pm. Admission charge. Metro: Camp Nou.

Gràcia

Once an independent village, in many ways Gràcia still feels separate from Barcelona. Its narrow streets and quaint squares are a nightmare to drive through (don't even try it) but make it one of the city's best places for pub crawls and tapas nights. Search out the Plaça del Sol, the Plaça Rius i Taulet or the Plaça de la Virreina for tapas bars and a lively atmosphere at night.
Metro: Fontana.

Parc Güell and Casa-Museu Gaudí

Gaudí intended the Parc Güell to be something like a modern-day gated community, with houses, a couple of shops and even a school. The plan

The fantasy architecture of the Parc Güell

failed, but the work he began was turned into what would become one of Barcelona's best-loved parks, a place with colourful mosaic benches, enchanting paths to discover and amazing city views. Be sure to take your picture next to the mosaic lizard at the entrance, which has become a symbol of Barcelona. In cool weather, walking the shady paths (there are more than 3km/2 miles of them) is a great option.

Near the entrance is the house Gaudí lived in for much of his later life. It's now a museum showcasing furniture designed by the architect, along with some personal belongings that give you an insight into the life of this very private man.
Casa-Museu Gaudí. Parc Güell. Tel: 93 219 3811. Open: Oct–Mar 10am–6pm, Apr–Sept 10am–8pm. Admission charge. Metro: Lesseps.

Tibidabo and Collserola

Rising above Barcelona are the Collserola mountains, low green hills criss-crossed with paths perfect for jogging, biking or just enjoying a slow stroll. One of these mountains is Tibidabo (Latin for 'to thee will I give', referring to the temptation of Christ on the mountain), which is topped with a smallish funfair that won't give you big thrills but is an entertaining way to spend a Saturday. Just beside the entrance is a rather cold-looking basilica, which was ordered to be built by Franco to remind the city of its sins. Needless to say, it's not the city's most popular church.

Near the funfair is the Torre de Collserola, a looming communications tower designed by Norman Foster. Ride to the top for unbeatable views of the city, though be warned that on hazy days you won't see much detail.

You can reach the base of the park and the tower with Tramvía Blau (Blue Tram), which leaves from the Avinguda del Tibidabo FCG rail station every 15–30 minutes.

Funfair. Plaça Tibidabo. Tel: 93 211 7942. Open: July–Aug Mon–Thur midday–10pm, Fri–Sun midday–11pm; June & Sept Sat–Sun midday–9pm; rest of year Sat–Sun midday–6pm. Admission charge.

Torre de Collserola. Carretera de Vallvidrera al Tibidabo. Tel: 93 406 9354. Open: June–Sept daily 11am–8pm; Oct–May daily 11am–6pm. Admission charge.

One of Gràcia's village squares

Montjuïc

Barcelona's big green lung, the low mountain of Montjuïc is a fantastic park-like area that feels miles away from the bustle of the city. Come up here to jog, see great panoramic views of Barcelona or visit some of the museums on and around the mountain.

Caixa Forum

Barcelona's newest museum, the Caixa Forum is housed in a refurbished textile factory and offers continuously changing exhibits of modern and contemporary art ranging from painting and sculpture to photography and video. There's also a great media library, which has magazines, music and movies.

Avinguda Marquès de Comillas 6–8. Tel: 93 476 8600. Open: Tue–Sun 10am–8pm. Free. Metro: Espanya.

Fundació Joan Miró

A broad collection of works by Catalan artist Joan Miró forms the basis of this fantastic museum. Tapestries, paintings, drawings and sculptures, most using Miró's trademark bright colours and simple

The imposing Palau Nacional, home of the Museu Nacional d'Art de Catalunya

Montjuïc is perfect for strolling

and trees from a variety of Mediterranean climates.

Dr. Font i Quer 2. Tel: 93 426 4935; www.jardibotanic.bcn.es. Open: Apr–Oct 10am–8pm, Nov–Mar 10am–5pm. Admission charge. Metro: Espanya.

Museu Nacional d'Art de Catalunya (National Museum of Catalan Art)

This is the place to see great Catalan art from the 18th and 19th centuries. There is also an excellent collection of Romanesque art, much of it originally housed in churches across the Catalan countryside. The museum is housed in the splendid Palau Nacional, built here for the 1888 World Fair.

Palau Nacional, Parc de Montjuïc. Tel. 93 622 0376; www.mnac.es. Open: Tue–Sat 10am–7pm, Sun 10am–2.30pm. Admission charge. Metro: Espanya.

Poble Espanyol

A mock Spanish village designed for the 1929 World Fair, the Poble Espanyol (literally, 'Spanish Village') is a rather kitsch but fun tourist attraction. More than two dozen artists and artisans have workshops here, making it a great place to buy locally made jewellery, toys, clothing, leather goods, paintings and sculpture. There are also several good restaurants and, at night, dance clubs.

Marquès de Comillas. Tel: 93 508 6300; www.poble-espanyol.com. Open: Mon 9am–8pm, Tue–Thur 9am–2am, Fri–Sat 9am–4am, Sun 9am–midnight. Admission charge. Metro: Espanya.

symbols, are all included in the collection. Temporary exhibits of mainly contemporary art are held here too, and there is a smart café perfect for a snack or coffee. The museum building itself, a striking white construction inspired by traditional Mediterranean forms, was built by Catalan architect Josep Lluís Sert.

Parc de Montjuïc. Tel: 91 443 9470; www.bcn.fjmiro.es. Open: Oct–June Tue–Sat 10am–7pm (8pm July–Sept), Thur 10am–9.30pm, Sun 10am–2.30pm. Admission charge. Metro: Espanya.

Jardí Botànic (Botanic Garden)

A pleasant and well-organised park, this is a great place to stroll among plants

Around Barcelona

The coast and green interior just north of Barcelona are within easy reach of the city and are popular places for short escapes. Find your way to one of the beaches, hike around the Parc Natural de Montseny or get away from it all at one of the historic spas in the Caldes de Montbui. Just 50 km (30 miles) from Barcelona are the rolling vineyards of El Penedès, one of Spain's top wine regions. Sparkling cava is made here, as are top whites and reds.

NORTH OF BARCELONA
Caldes de Montbui and Spa Country

Caldes de Montbui is a historic thermal village just 30km (18 1/2 miles) outside Barcelona. In the days of the Romans it was already a popular spot for bathing and was recognised for the healing powers of its natural spring waters. It's now home to several excellent modern spas, some centuries old and others built with lovely Modernist touches. The waters here are supposed to help relieve stress, joint problems and obesity, among other ills.
Tourist Office. Plaça de la Font del Lleó 20. Tel: 93 865 4140.

Costa del Maresme

Stretching 50km (30 miles) up the Mediterranean coast, the Costa del Maresme is known for its long, golden beaches. These beaches would likely be even more popular if it weren't for the railway line that runs just along the sea all the way from Barcelona to La Costa

Brava. Nevertheless, beach towns like **Arenys de Mar**, **Calella**, **Sant Pol de Mar**, **Canet de Mar** and **Pineda de Mar**

The Barcelona region

offer accessible beaches that are just a hop from Barcelona.

The largest town in the area is **Mataró**, best known for its beach and leisure port but also home to a few important monuments, like the baroque Basílica de Santa María.

Montseny

The Parc Natural de Montseny is a lovely green area offering beautiful scenery and excellent hiking options. A massif covered in low vegetation, Montseny is divided into two halves by the Tordera River. To the west is the Pla de la Calma (Calm Prairie), and to the west is the Turó de l'Home (Hill of the Man). Both offer plenty

of options for enjoying the great outdoors. Historic towns are dotted about the mountainside; villages like La Garriga, El Figaró and El Brull make great resting points in between mountain hikes. Buses travel to and among several Montseny towns. *Information Office. Carrer Major 6, Arbúcies. Tel: 93 847 5102; www. diba.es/parcs/montseny/montseny.htm*

Sant Celoni

Considered the gateway to the Parc Natural de Montseny, the small town of Sant Celoni makes a good base for excursions in the area, with a solid selection of hotels and restaurants. The town actually owes most of its

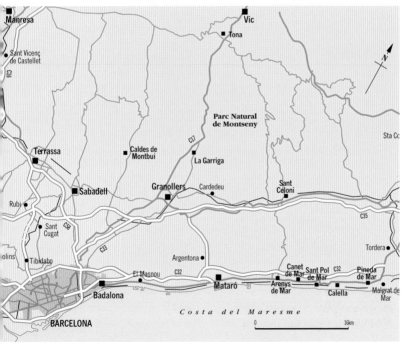

The Basílica de Santa María in Vilafranca

renown to one of the restaurants here, El Racó de Can Fabes, a cosy establishment that's been awarded three Michelin stars. The famed chef, Santi Santamaría, is known for his use of fresh local products and his perfect presentation of dishes based on traditional Catalan cooking.

PENEDÈS WINE COUNTRY
Vilafranca del Penedès

The capital of a *comarca* (county), Vilafranca is the centre of the wine business here and has an interesting medieval centre that's easily walkable. Be sure to visit the Gothic Basílica de Santa María on the Plaça de Jaume I. Across from the church is the interesting Museu del Vi (*see below*).

The town is famous for its wine, but it's also known for its outstanding human castle team (*see pp76–7*), which is widely considered the best in Catalonia. During fiestas and festivals *casteller* exhibitions are held on the Plaça de la Vila in the centre. This plaza wears a proud plaque declaring it the *plaça més casteller* (best *casteller* plaza) of Catalonia.

On Saturday mornings, Vilafranca hosts a massive produce and flea market that many people consider the best in all Catalonia. You can buy everything here from fish and veggies, live chickens and ducks to clothing, kitchen utensils and hardware.

Vilafranca Tourist Office. Carrer Cort 14. Tel: 93 892 0358; www.vilafranca.com. Guided tours of the town are available.

Museu del Vi

Get a handle on the Penedès region's long winemaking history in this interesting museum. Old bodega equipment, an interesting bottle collection, art and intricate dioramas depicting the local lifestyle form part of the exhibition. At the end you'll get a free glass of wine to taste.
Plaça Jaume 1. Tel: 93 890 0582. Admission charge.

Torres winery

Penedès owes its national and international acclaim in large part to the enterprising winemaker Miguel Torres, whose innovations in winemaking started the modern wine boom in the region. Visit the winery, where you'll see a video, go on a fun train tour around the facilities and end with a tasting.

Bodegas Torres, Pacs del Penedès. Tel: 93 817 7400; www.torres.es. Open: Mon–Sat 9am–5pm, Sun 9am–1pm. Free admission.

Sant Sadurní d'Anoia

The capital of cava (sparkling wine), Sant Sadurní is the eternal rival of its neighbour Vilafranca. Though the town itself is not much of an attraction, there are several cava producers worth visiting. The tourist office has full details, but you can start with those listed on our Penedès tour (*see next page*).

Tourist Office. Plaça Ajuntament 1. Tel: 93 891 0325.

Olérdola

A fascinating archaeological site off the C-15 highway, hilltop Olérdola is a tiny town where you can see remains of Iberian, Roman and medieval settlements. At times it's confusing to discern exactly what you're looking at, but on the site you'll find ruins of pre-Roman Iberian houses, Roman walls and watchtower and a large Romanesque church that dominates them all. There's also a small archaeology museum with artefacts found here.

Museu d'Arqueologia de Catalunya – Olérdola. Castell d'Olérdola. Tel: 93 890 1420. Open: mid-Oct–mid-Mar Tue–Fri 10am–2pm & 3–6pm, Sat–Sun 10am–4pm; mid-Mar–mid-Oct Tue–Fri 10am–2pm & 3–8pm, Sat–Sun 10am–2pm & 3–8pm. Admission charge.

The old method of wine pressing on display at a Penedès winery

Tour: Penedès wine country

Of the dozens of small cavas and bodegas that dot Penedès, only a handful are open for visits or tastings. Yet even if you don't make it inside many wineries, driving through the vineyard-streaked countryside is a joy.

1 Vilafranca del Penedès

It's a good idea to start off your wine tour with a visit to Vilafranca's Museu del Vi to get a good overview of wine and winemaking in the area. When you're ready to hit the road, take the C-15 highway (a major road that runs through the centre of town) towards Igualada. After 11km (7 miles) green vineyards come rolling into view.

2 Jean Leon

Turn right on a small highway towards BV-2153 towards El Plá. A sign on your

left will lead the way up a dirt road to Jean Leon. At this unique winery you'll learn about the winery's founder, a Spanish immigrant who made it big in the US, founding the famous restaurant La Scala and finally returning to Spain to create his own wines. The modern visitor's centre, where you can see a video about the winery and visit a small museum, offers incredible views over Penedès.

Pago Jean Leon, Torrelavit. Tel: 93 899 5512; www.jeanleon.com. Open: by appointment. Admission charge, includes tasting of two wines.

3 Codorníu

Out of Jean Leon turn left and continue on the BV-2153 and follow signs towards Sant Sadurní d'Anoia, taking a right and then your first left, which will take you into the town centre. Just past the centre is Codorníu, one of the area's oldest and best cava producers. The tour leads you through the winery, designed by the Modernist architect Josep Puig i Cadafalch, and takes you on a fun train ride through the underground cellars.

Avinguda Jaume Codorníu, Sant Sadurni d'Anoia. Tel: 93 818 3232; www.codorniu.es. Open: Mon–Fri 9am–5pm, Sat–Sun 9am–1pm. Admission charge, includes glass of cava.

4 Sant Sadurní d'Anoia

As you drive through this capital of cava, 1.5km (1 mile) south, you may want to stop for a quick peek at the Església Parroquial (parish church), a mainly Gothic building in the town centre. In early October Sant Sadurní hosts a cava festival, a week of fun events focussing on the bubbly beverage.

Tourist Office. Carrer Hospital 26. Tel: 93 891 3188; www.santsadurni.org. Open: Tue–Fri 10am–2pm & 5–7pm, Sat–Sun 10am–2pm.

5 Freixenet

Head south 1.5km (1 mile) to visit Freixenet. This mammoth cava producer has its winery beside the Sant Sadurní railway line, so it's a very accessible place. The tour starts with a video that explains the history of the Freixenet family; it goes on to give a tour of the cellars and a tasting.

Carrer Joan Sala 2, Sant Sadurní d'Anoia. Tel: 93 891 7000; www.freixenet.es. Open: tours given hourly Mon–Thur 11am–1pm & 3–4.30pm, Fri–Sun 10am–1pm. Free admission.

6 Sant Pau d'Ordal

After a long tour you deserve a rest, and this is one of the best spots for it. In the very centre of Sant Pau d'Ordal, local favourite Cal Xim offers hearty, home-style regional foods and a wide variety of local wines and cavas.

Plaça Subirats 5, Sant Pau d'Ordal. Tel: 93 899 3147. Open lunch only.

The Codorníu winery, designed in Modernist style by Josep Puig i Cadafalch

The mountain-top monastery in Montserrat

MONTSERRAT

Montserrat, a huge massif that pops without warning out of the low hills of the Catalan countryside, is the unofficial symbol of Catalonia. Home to the region's patron saint, La Moreneta (the little brown one), and a place of pilgrimage for nearly a millennium, this strangely shaped mountain is the spiritual heart of Catalonia. In English its name means 'serrated mountain', an apt description of the rounded peaks that make its top look like a saw from a distance.

The Benedictine Monastery of Montserrat, nestled among the bulbous peaks of the mountain, is still a pilgrimage site, but it's also one of Catalonia's top tourist attractions and is well equipped to handle the more than 2.5 million visitors who arrive each year by tour bus, car and the monastery's own scenic cable car.

You can get here by train from Barcelona. FGC trains leave the Plaça d'Espanya railway station every two hours daily and take an hour to reach the Aeri de Montserrat. From there you'll take a cable car to the monastery. The last train leaves Aeri de Montserrat at 7.30pm, and the return fare (including cable car) is approx. €12. Alternatively, you can take the train to Monistrol and there catch a *cremallera* ('zipper' or small-gauge mountain train) that rushes you up the mountainside. The price is about the same.

Oficina de Turisme de Montserrat. Plaça de la Creu, Montserrat. Tel: 93 877 7701; www.montserratvisita.com. Open: Apr–Oct daily 9am–7pm; Nov–Mar daily 9am–6pm. Free admission.

The Basílica and around

Be sure to enter the Basilica, a 15th-century church dripping with gold, and walk up the stairs behind the altar to the Camarín de la Virgen, where the wooden statue of La Moreneta sits. According to legend, young shepherds found the dark-coloured Romanesque statue of the Virgin Mary in a cave on the mountain. The Basilica is always most crowded at 1pm, when the monastery's celebrated boys' choir sings Mass. They sing again at 7.10pm, and at 12 noon on Sundays.

La Moreneta, the black Virgin of Montserrat

THE LEGEND OF LA MORENETA

The small black statue of the Virgin holding baby Jesus has a legendary past that blurs the line between fact and fiction.

Supposedly, the statue was carved in Jerusalem and brought to Catalonia by St Peter. When the Muslims invaded, it was hidden in a cave on Montserrat mountain. Centuries later a group of shepherds saw a light coming out of the cave and discovered La Moreneta inside. When local priests loaded her on to a cart, the cart wouldn't budge. After trying again and again to move the statue, they understood that their struggles were a sign from the Virgin telling them to leave her on the mountain. So a small stone chapel was built near the spot, and she never left Montserrat.

Years later the ornate Basilica and monastery that now dominate Montserrat were created. But you can still visit the rebuilt Santa Cova (Holy Cave) where La Moreneta was found. A small replica of the statue sits here on a rugged stone altar.

A string of boutique-ish shops near the monastery's entrance give a commercial feel to the place but they offer a good selection of souvenirs and local specialities such as honey. Above the shops is an audiovisual presentation that recounts the daily life of the 80 or so monks who live and work in the monastery.

Basilica. Open: 7.30am–7.30pm.
Camarín de la Virgen.
Open: 8.30–10.30am & 12–6.30pm;
July–Sept also open 7.30–8.30pm.
Audiovisual presentation. Open: mid-Sept–end May 9am–6pm; rest of year 9am–7.45pm. Admission charge.

Montserrat's famous boys' choir

Museu de Montserrat

Below the Basilica is the interesting Museu de Montserrat, where you can see an excellent collection of Catalan artists ranging from Modernist painters like Ramon Casas to later artists such as Salvador Dalí. There's also a collection of religious art from Italy and Spain and an enlightening section on the importance of Montserrat in Catholic symbolism and the Church. The museum entrance is just below the Plaça de Santa María. *Monastery Museum. Tel: 93 877 7701. Open: Oct–Dec Mon–Fri 10am–6pm, Sat–Sun 9.30am–6.30pm; July–mid-Sept 10am–7pm. Admission charge.*

The mountain

The true beauty of Montserrat lies in its incredible natural environment. Its unique peaks were formed by erosion after the softer land that surrounded this mass of rock sank into the ground, leaving Montserrat exposed in all its jagged glory. Trails ramble throughout; the most accessible start near the monastery itself. Take a funicular to Santa Cova, the cave where the statue of the Black Virgin was supposedly found. Another funicular goes to the hermitage of Sant Joan, where a steep trail with great views leads back down to the monastery. Numerous chapels, most of them abandoned and in ruins, surround the monastery and make for good hiking destinations. Rock climbing is another popular activity on the mountain. The on-site tourist office has trail maps.

Parc Natural de la Muntanya de Montserrat

Beyond the monastery is a wide expanse of protected parkland full of even more trails. This is a popular place for excursionists and rock climbers, and there are several facilities for them, including a mountain refuge where you can spend the night. Get more details at the monastery information office. *www.parcsdecatalunya.net*

SITGES AND EL GARRAF

Sophisticated Sitges is the most popular resort near Barcelona. Vilanova, just a few kilometres down the beach, is a working fishermen's town where you can get some of the best seafood Catalonia has to offer.

Santa Cova

Montserrat's jagged peaks

Sitges is the most popular resort close to Barcelona

Garraf

The main sight in this tiny coastal resort, other than its cove beach (which is lovely but overcrowded), is the Modernist Celler de Garraf, designed by Gaudí. It's now open only for private functions, but you can appreciate its unusual forms and daring design from the C-31 highway that snakes past town.

Sitges

One of the few coastal resorts that's managed to keep its own personality in the face of tourism, Sitges is an upmarket beach town known for its great nightlife and thriving gay community. Most people come to lounge on the golden beaches here; while small, they're very clean with calm waves and easy access to beach-side bars and activities like paddle boats and windsailing.

The town centre is full of shops and restaurants. There are several unique clothing stores here and dozens of galleries selling work by local artists. You'll also find locally made jewellery and a fantastic selection of shoe shops. A few museums round out the cultural offerings. Sitges' immaculate Passeig Maritim (seaside boulevard) is great for jogging or roller skating by day, and it becomes a romantic (if often crowded) boulevard by night.
Tourist Office. Carrer Sínia Morera 1. Tel: 93 894 5004; www.sitges.org.

Museums

Museu Cau Ferrat (*Carrer Fonollar. Tel: 93 894 0364. Closed Mon. Admission charge.*) The former home of resident artist Santiago Rusiñol, this charmingly decorated house perched on the cliff edge was a meeting place for Modernist artists and is now a museum with works by El Greco, Picasso and others.

Museu Romántic (*Carrer Sant Gaudenci. Tel: 93 894 2969. Closed Mon. Admission charge.*) If you're interested in 19th-century life in Sitges, take a look at this small museum in the town centre where you'll see exhibits on everyday life in those days.

Palau Maricel (*Carrer Fonollar. Tel: 93 894 0364. Closed Mon. Admission charge.*) A Modernist extravaganza, this former hospital is covered head to toe in colourful tiles and mosaics. Concerts and other special events are held here in summer.

La Punta

The main church, Sant Bartolomeu i Santa Tecla, is the crowning glory of the seafront and is perched on a rocky cliff as though daring some summer storm to knock it over. Though the steps leading up to the church have been washed away more than once, the building itself has never been touched. Locals say that fishermen's wives used to climb the bell tower to watch the horizon for their husbands' return.

Vilanova i la Geltrú

The next community down the coast, Vilanova is a working-class *poble* (town) where you can find some of Catalonia's best seafood restaurants. Stroll down the Rambla that cuts through the town centre and stop by for a peek in the Biblioteca-Museu Victor Balaguer, which holds some interesting artwork.
Tourist Office. Plaça de la Vila 10. Tel: 93 893 5555; www.vilanova.org

Sant Bartolomeu; Santa Tecla

Walk: Garraf coast

This lovely walk takes you beside hidden coves, lapping waves and even a nude beach or two as it leads you from through the town of Sitges to neighbouring Vilanova.

Allow two hours for the walk, more if you plan to swim, sunbathe or picnic along the way.

1 Sitges, railway station

The walk begins in front of the railway station, which is an easy 30-minute ride from Barcelona. From the station head down Carrer Francesc Gomà; when it ends turn right on to Carrer Jesús and soon you'll find yourself in the town's small but central main plaza, Cap de la Vila. At the pharmacy turn left on to Carrer Major and follow the curving street until you reach the Ajuntament (Town Hall).

2 Passeig Marítim

Walk the length of the maritime promenade, passing beaches, seaside bars and restaurants, and some gorgeous waterfront homes. In about 35 minutes you'll reach a large hotel at the end of the promenade. Head down to Còdols beach and cross the bed of the Ribes stream. Continue on the dirt road that leads down to a nightclub and a large car park.

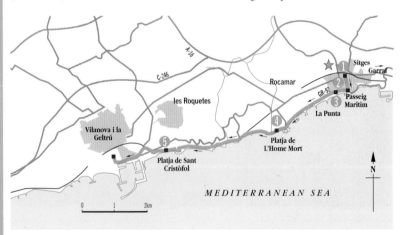

3 GR-92 trail

Cross the car park and in the far right corner (near the train track) you'll see the pickup for the GR-92 trail. This trail runs the length of the Catalan coast; it's possible to follow it all the way to France. If you get really ambitious, you can follow this same trail as it becomes the international E-10, which links the Mediterranean with the Baltic! For now, just start down this narrow but well-marked path, which takes a meandering route running almost parallel to the railway line.

4 Platja de L'Home Mort (Dead Man's Beach)

The trail winds around fragrant thyme and rosemary bushes and other scrubby brush as it makes its way over the rocky terrain of the Garraf. There are countless coves along the path, most of them accessible only by sea. You can make your way out on to the rock outcrops for great views and picnic spots. In some areas, you'll even be able to pick your way down to the water for a dip. Several of the larger beaches here are popular with nudists and gay men, though mid-week you'll probably find them deserted.

5 Platja de Sant Cristòfol (St Christopher's Beach)

In a little over an hour you'll come to the small Platja de Sant Cristòfol. Here the trail becomes a paved road that leads into Vilanova. Follow it until you cross a small bridge over a stream bed. Now take the first right, and in less than 10 minutes you'll find yourself at Vilanova's railway station. From here you can take the train back to Sitges.

Easy strolling on Sitges' Passeig Maritim

Walk: Garraf coast

Castellers

Perhaps Catalans have a penchant for danger, or maybe they're just brave. There seem to be few other explanations of the thrilling tradition of the *castellers* (human castle builders). These teams of men, women and children (aged 5 to 65) get together and, just for fun, stack themselves one on top of the other to create swaying pyramids that rise up to ten bodies in the air. Yes, they fall sometimes. Yes, it looks incredibly dangerous. But the town's *castellers* are revered the way local football heroes are, and the *castellers* tradition is beloved as a symbol of Catalan unity and strength.

During fiestas and special events, crowds pack into town plazas to get a glimpse of the show, which can last all morning as two or three competing *castellers* teams try to outdo each other, building bigger and taller *castells* as the morning wears on.

A *castell* begins when the clarinet-like music of the *gralles* hushes the crowd. The team, which can number in the hundreds, first forms a tight mass of bodies, or *pinya*, on the ground, and then the climbers start their work. Four stout men called *baixos* (bases) intertwine their arms tightly and clench their jaws in concentration to form the first level. They'll be supporting the weight of some two dozen people on their shoulders, and as a foundation anchors a house they'll keep the pyramid above them strong and steady.

Slowly others climb above the *baixos*, their grimy black bare feet searching for hips, shoulders and

The beginnings of a *castell*

The *gralles* heralds the beginning of the *castell* building

heads to use as steps. The second level forms another tight circle on top, concentrating on keeping balance so that the next round of climbers can in turn make it on to their shoulders. The tower grows ever taller into the air, each storey made up of bodies smaller and lighter than the one before it until mere children are scrambling up.

Casteller supporters argue that human castles are less dangerous than contact sports like football or basketball, but 8 metres (26 ft) or more off the ground is never the safest place to be. Yet amazingly, few serious injuries are reported, and only one *casteller* has died in the line of duty in the past 100 years.

Human castles have a long and proud, if confused, history in Catalonia. There are those that claim the tradition came from the Romans, who got it from the Greeks. Some say it evolved from a religious dance that portrayed Christ rising into heaven. One version claims the 'sport' has its roots in a war technique to climb into walled cities. Another says a group of Catalans trapped inside a fort invented the castle as a way to scale the wall and send someone for help. And some say building human towers was a way Catalan cowboys entertained themselves at night.

What is certain is that human castles in their modern form have been in Catalonia for nearly 200 years, and that in that time they have come to represent the community and teamwork, the competition and desire for victory, the stability and sensibility, the very essence, of a Catalan.

A completed *castell*

Southern Catalonia

Southern Catalonia stretches along the Mediterranean coast from Tarragona down to the marshy Ebro River Delta, encompassing pristine natural areas, dry coastal mountains and seaside resorts like Salou and Cambrils. Much of this part of Catalonia is rural, and the people depend heavily on the olive, almond and grape crops, all of which are famous for their excellent quality.

The largest city, Tarragona, was a Roman stronghold that has some of Iberia's best ancient monuments. From there you can explore the coastal resorts nearby or head inland to the hilly Priorat region, where some of Spain's best red wine is made. In the southern tip of Catalonia you'll find a fabulous bird habitat in the Ebro River Delta Nature Park.

TARRAGONA

In its prime, Roman Tarraco was the capital of the province of Hispania Citerior and the second most important city in the Roman Empire. A large circus and an amphitheatre were the boisterous arenas for entertainment, two central forums provided a place for intellectual and political pursuits and a strong wall converted the city into a

Southern Catalonia

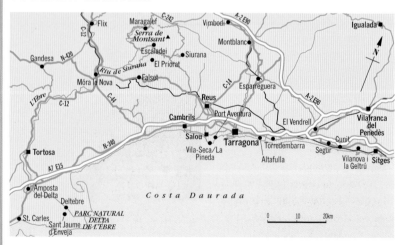

A small square in the heart of old Tarragona

fortress. The Emperor Augustus called Tarraco home for a time, as did Pontius Pilate (who was born here).

These days, Tarragona is often overlooked under the shadow of Barcelona and the many kilometres of sparkling beaches surrounding nearby, but its exciting history is still there to be seen in bits and pieces throughout the city.
Tarragona Tourist Office. Carrer Major 39; www.fut.es/~turisme. Tel: 97 725 0795. Open: Sept–June Mon–Sat 10am–2pm & 4–7pm, Sun 10am–2pm; July–Aug Mon–Fri 9am–9pm, Sat 9am–2pm & 4–9pm, Sun 10am–2pm.

Amfiteatre Romà

As the centre of Roman entertainment, the amphitheatre was an important part of Tarraco. The amphitheatre's floor is laced with tunnels and corridors that were used for gladiators and ferocious animals; these tunnels would have been covered with a wooden floor and trapdoors.

The ruins of a basilica fill one end of the amphitheatre.
Parc del Miracle. Tel: 97 724 2579; www.museutgn.com. Open: Easter–Oct 9am–9pm; Nov–Easter 9am–5pm, closed Mon. Admission charge.

Balcó del Mediterrani

Perhaps the prettiest spot in the city, the palm-lined 'Balcony of the Mediterranean' is a long plaza overlooking the sea. It sits at the end of the Rambla Nova, a busy strolling street that's lined with shops, bars and restaurants. Stick a few coins into the bright blue telescopes for a close-up of the rough hillsides that run alongside the sea.

Tarragona's cathedral dominates the city

Catedral de Tarragona

Tarragona's splendid 12th-century cathedral began as a Romanesque creation with five naves, a central apse and two secondary apses. The façade was added later, in the 15th century, and is a Gothic design with a fabulously detailed portal. Inside, the 15th-century altar (a work of Catalan master Pere Joan) is worth seeking out, but more interesting still is the peaceful cloister, which is filled with a garden and lined with delicate arches.

Plaça de la Seu. Tel: 97 723 8685. Open: mid-Mar–May 10am–1pm & 4–7pm; June–mid-Sept 10am–7pm; mid-Sept– mid-Nov 10am–5pm; mid-Nov–mid-Mar 10am–2pm. Admission charge.

Museu Nacional Arqueològic de Tarragona

This archaeological museum gives a solid overview of life in Roman Tarraco. From mosaics to wine jugs to children's toys, you'll find it all here. There's a large collection of Roman sculptures, though precious few of them show more than a couple of broken body parts. The collection is well presented, but if you can't read Catalan you'll miss out.

Plaça del Rei 5. Tel: 97 723 6209; www.mnat.es. Open: June–Sept 10am–8pm; Oct–May 9.30am–1.30pm & 3.30–7pm, Sun 10am–2pm, closed Mon. Admission charge.

Passeig Arqueològic

Take a stroll alongside Tarragona's ancient defensive walls, part of which date to the 3rd century BC. The walls, which once stretched 4km (2½ miles), were added to and strengthened through the Middle Ages and in the 18th century, so you'll see three distinct building styles. There is an interesting exhibit that details the walls' history and construction.

Avinguda de Catalunya. Tel: 97 724 5796; www.museutgn.org. Open: Easter–Oct 9am–9pm; Nov–Easter 9am–5pm, Sun 10am–3pm, closed Mon. Admission charge.

Beaches

Tarragona has decent city beaches, but they're a hike from the centre. Buses from the Rambla Nova can take you the 1km ($^1/_3$ mile) out to the Platja Arrabassada, which lies just up the coast or to the Platja Llarga, which is a bit further out. The Platja del Miracle is closer to town but not nearly as pleasant.

Pretori i Circ Romà

The 1st-century Roman circus and Pretori were originally built outside the city walls because of their size; the circus originally measured an impressive 290 × 115m (317 × 126yds) and was used for chariot races and other spectacles. The Pretori served many functions over the years, from a prison to a palace.

The most interesting part of the complex is the underground tunnel of the circus that ran right through underneath the stadium to give patrons easy access to their seats – a system surprisingly similar to that used by modern sports arenas. Also worthwhile is the panoramic view from the top of the Pretori.

Plaça del Rei and Rambla Vella. Tel: 97 723 0171; www.museutgn.org. Open Easter–Oct 9am–9pm; Nov–Easter 9am–7pm, closed Mon. Admission charge.

These sculptures were added to the cathedral façade in the 14th century

Walk: Old Tárraco

Close your eyes and imagine away the noise of modern Tarragona. Now picture a city full of stone, mosaics and tie-up sandals. This is a step back in time to the days when the Emperor Augustus called the city of Tarraco home and prime Saturday entertainment was a night out at the amphitheatre.

Allow one hour for the walk, a full day to enjoy all the sights.

1 Amfiteatre Romà

Start the Roman walk outside the amphitheatre. Even if you don't visit the site up close, there are great views from the Passeig de les Palmeres just outside the gate.

Contrary to popular belief, very few Christians were martyred in Roman amphitheatres, but Tarragona's amphitheatre was the site of one significant killing; the bishop Fructuosus and his two deacons were

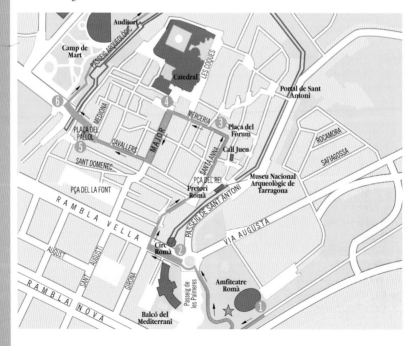

burned alive here in AD 259. Eventually a small basilica was built here to commemorate the martyrs; you can clearly see the ruins of the church even from outside the gate.

2 Pretori and Circ Romà

From the amphitheatre, head up the Rambla Vella to reach the entrance of the Roman praetorium. Walk through the complex and you'll come out on the Plaça del Rei. From here follow the Carrer Santa Ana to the Plaça del Fòrum.

3 Plaça del Fòrum

This sunny plaza was the site of Tarraco's forum, the area that served as the city's central square and once would have been a busy place full of scholars, merchants and townspeople. These days you'll really have to use your imagination to conjure up images of what this area might have looked like; all that is here now is a single ruined wall and a few boulders.

4 Carrer Major

Walk the length of the plaza and continue down Carrer Merceria. Turn left on to the bustling shopping street Carrer Major and take the second right on to Carrer Cavallers.

5 Plaça del Pallol

At the end of Carrer Cavallers is the intimate Plaça del Pallol, a charming square where you'll see parts of the old Roman wall and a few thick Roman gates. Cars still come and go out of the main wall gate here; pedestrians have to be careful when passing through.

6 Passeig Arqueològic

Finish the walk by taking a slow tour along the Archaeological Promenade, a kilometre- ($^1/_3$ mile-) long path that runs alongside the city walls. The inner walls are of Roman origin, while the outer walls (that indeed look made for simply strolling, as you are doing) were constructed much later, during the War of the Spanish Succession.

The Circ Romà forms part of the ancient city

One of Altafulla's medieval streets

THE COSTA DAURADA

The coast surrounding Tarragona is lined with golden sand and dotted with some of the best resort towns Catalonia has to offer. Whether you're looking for a quiet town perfect for families or a lively resort packed with nightlife options, you'll find it along this 'Golden Coast'. All towns listed here are off the N-340 highway or the AP-7 motorway, which run parallel to one another.

Altafulla

Some 10km (6 miles) of Tarragona, low-key Altafulla is a family resort with a charming medieval centre. You'll know you're in the Med when you're strolling by the whitewashed houses and dripping geraniums of the centre. Also check out

the 13th-century hilltop castle, the Castell de Tamarit.
Tourist Office. Plaça del Vents.
Tel: 97 765 0752; www.altafulla-web.org

Cambrils

Like so many other resorts here, Cambrils was just a humble fishing village until a few decades ago, when tourism discovered this pristine town and filled it with hotels, bars and restaurants. Yet it's still a fishing village at heart and you'll find fabulous seafood restaurants tucked into its maze-like medieval centre. If you're interested in learning more about the town, stop by for a quick visit at one of the branches of the Museu d'Història

de Cambrils; you can get more information at the tourist office.
Tourist Office. Passeig Palmeres. Tel: 97 779 2307; www.cambrils.org

Cunit

Another charming coastal village, Cunit is a quiet place that has yet to see the all-out tourist boom of towns like Salou. Come here to relax on the beach or to search out the few local restaurants that serve authentic Catalan cuisine. The 18th-century church of St Christopher was built atop Roman ruins and makes for an interesting visit.
Tourist Office. Carrer Major 2. Tel: 97 767 4080.

La Pineda

Perfect for families, quiet La Pineda is just a few kilometres from the frenzy of Salou and the busy Port Aventura theme park, but it feels like another world. The soft sandy beaches are clean, wide and known as some of the safest in the area. The town itself has a beautiful seaside promenade and a solid selection of restaurants and bars,

The beach at Cambrils

though for some real action you had better head to the nearby resorts of Salou and Cambrils.
Tourist Office. Carrer del Patró, Vila-Seca. Tel: 97 739 0362.

Universal Mediterranean–Port Aventura

The biggest and best theme park in Catalonia, Universal Mediterranean is a mega-complex with a sprawling water park, a themed attractions park, hotels and more. Race down the slides at Costa Caribe, the water park, or ride the super Dragon Kahn roller coaster at Port Aventura.
Universal Mediterranean–Port Aventura. Tel: 97 777 9090; www.portaventura.com. Open (hours may change, check with park): Apr–June 10am–7pm; July–mid-Sept 10am–midnight; mid-Sept–Nov 10am–7pm; Dec–Mar hours vary, usually open weekends only. Admission charge.

Salou

A fabulously long, golden beach is the star attraction of this popular resort town, whose winter population of under 10,000 swells tremendously in August. The beach itself is one of the best in Catalonia, and it draws throngs of sun-worshippers from all over northern Europe, the UK and Spain. With the abundance of Irish pubs, English taverns and German eateries, you may feel like you never left home.
Tourist Office. Passeig Jaume I 4. Tel: 97 735 0102.

Siurana, perched dramatically on a clifftop

EL PRIORAT

This dry, rocky region west of Tarragona is a world away from the resorts and touristy towns of coastal Catalonia. A rural land where nearly all the buildings are made of stone and people still harvest grapes by hand, Priorat feels like a sleepy place but is really one of Catalonia's most innovative wine regions, producing strong, pricey reds that have become some of Spain's most popular.

The *comarca* (county) of Priorat is divided into two DOs (denominations of origin, similar to French *appellations controlées*), Priorat and Montsant. The latter forms a ring around the former, and both are known for their rich, slightly mineral wines. This region is also known for its fantastic olives, olive oil and almonds.

Escaladei

Escaladei is a rather sleepy town focused on the production and sale of wine, but a kilometre (¹/₃ mile) beyond the town centre is the 12th-century Cartoixa d'Escaladei, the first Carthusian monastery on the Iberian peninsula. The monastery was abandoned in the 1830s and is now in ruins, but there are regular guided visits. You can wander through the now-ceilingless halls of the monastery; inside, a fountain here and an arch there are all that remain of the original structure. For visitors' benefit, an example of the monks' living quarters has been rebuilt. Since Carthusian monks lived in solitude and silence, each one had his own cell, with a chapel, a study, a garden, a bedroom and a kitchen.

Escaladei. Tel: 97 782 7006.
Open: Oct–May Tue–Sun 10am–1.30pm
& 3–5.30pm; June–Sept 10am–1.30pm
& 4–7.30pm. Admission charge.

Falset

The county capital, Falset is a small town with an historic centre and a few sights worth seeking out. The historic centre is pretty, if unremarkable (though it does have the dubious distinction of being the last place in Catalonia to host a public hanging). Just outside town, in the direction of Reus, the Ermita de Sant Gregori (1369) is a plain brick chapel built into the mountainside. The soft, red rock has been moulded by rain, wind and time, and it moves in waves. Natural rock sculptures surround the chapel, and the views of the vineyard-filled valley and the town of Falset are something special.

Priorat Tourist Office. Carrer Sant Marcel 2, Falset. Tel: 97 783 1023; www.priorat.org

Serra de Montsant Parc Natural

Dominating the landscape of Priorat are the bare rock walls of the Montsant mountains. Popular with hikers and rock climbers, this sparse landscape has a unique beauty. Get information about hiking and biking trails from the information office.

Information Office. Carrer Major 4, Morera de Montsant. Tel: 977 82 7092.

Siurana

Looking out over the region from its perch atop a rock cliff, this tiny town is one of Priorat's most beautiful. Wander its twisted old streets and be sure to visit the Arab castle, the last Muslim stronghold in Catalonia. According to legend the castle's queen committed suicide by jumping off the mountaintop when the castle was seized by Catalan leader Ramón Berenguer IV in 1153.

St Gregory's Hermitage, built into the living rock

Tour: El Priorat

Small, family-owned wineries fill Priorat, but very few are open to visitors. Follow this route through the terraced vineyards of the region to seek out a few of the places that are open to the public, but bear in mind that you will need to make reservations several days in advance for any wineries that you plan to visit.

Allow two hours for the circuit, more if you plan to make stops.

1 Falset

Start your tour in Falset, where you can visit the Falset-Marçà Bodega, a cooperative that falls under the Montsant DO. The cellar itself is a Modernist creation built in 1919 by César Martinell, one of Gaudí's students. You'll find the bodega's office cum shop on the main road (N-420) that cuts through town.

Falset–Marçà Bodega. Avinguda del Priorat, Falset. Tel: 97 783 0105.

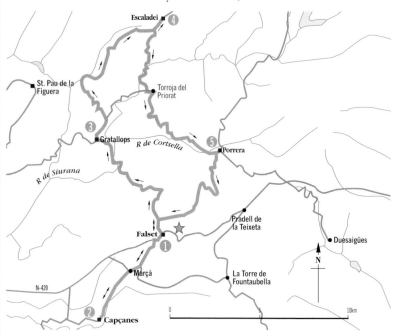

Open weekends only, tours only given to groups, so call ahead to find out if there is a group you can join. Admission charge.

2 Capçanes

Take a quick detour south on the TV-3002 towards Marçà and continue past the town to the cooperative of Capçanes, which makes one of Spain's few kosher wines. Though technically it's only open for tours at weekends at noon, you can call ahead and request a private tour.
Capçanes. Plaça de la Cooperativa, Capçanes. Tel: 97 717 8319.
Open: weekends 12pm for tour (reservation required), shop open: Mon–Fri 9am–1pm & 3–5pm, Sat–Sun 10am–2pm.
Admission charge.

3 Gratallops

Return to Falset, cross town and take the T-710 north towards Gratallops. This scenic drive takes you along the Siurana River. In Gratallops you can visit the well-known Costers del Siurana winery, which makes Clos d'Obac and other great wines.

Vine-covered terraces of El Priorat

Costers del Siurana. Camí Manyanetes, Pol 11. Tel: 97 783 9276; www.costersdelsiurana.com. Open: daily but call ahead to arrange a visit. Free admission.

4 Escaladei

Continue on the T-710 out of town and take your second right on to the T-702 towards Escaladei. In town there are several wineries and an excellent wine shop. Open to visitors are the top-quality La Conreria d'Scala Dei and Cellers d'Scala Dei.
La Conreria d'Scala Dei. Carrer Mitja Galta 32. Tel: 649 935 610 (mobile phone). Open: Mon–Sat after 12 noon by reservation only. Admission charge.
Cellers d'Scala Dei. Rambla Cartoixa. Tel: 97 782 7027 or 97 782 7173. Open: daily by reservation only. Free admission.

5 Porrera and Falset

From here take the scenic TP-7403, a windy road not for the faint-hearted! When you reach Porrera (a town that has several visitable wineries as well) turn right on to the equally curvy T-740, which leads back to Falset.

THE CURSE OF PHYLLOXERA

Before the insect-borne *Phylloxera* disease wiped out vineyards all over Europe at the end of the 1800s, Priorat was a prestigious region whose wines were solicited by connoisseurs from France and other countries. Priorat did recover to some extent from the blow, but it satisfied itself with making mass-market wines and did not regain its reputation for quality until the 1990s.

Tour: El Priorat

Catalan wine

Penedès and Priorat may be the best-known Catalan wine regions, but they're not the only ones. Winemaking has a long history in Catalonia, dating back to the days of the Romans, and regions throughout the land make excellent wines.

Alella

Just north of Barcelona, this small coastal region covers just 500 hectares (1,250 acres) but has a long winemaking history. The very existence of these vineyards is constantly threatened by Barcelona's urban sprawl, but the region still produces tasty whites known for being light and mellow. Find more information at *www.doalella.com*

Conca de Barberà

An excellent white wine region in central Catalonia, Conca de Barberà is nestled amid two river valleys, the Francolí and the Anguera. Traditional white varieties like Garnatxa blanca, Macabeu and Parellada (all local varieties) make up the bulk of production, though a few top quality red wines are beginning to be made here as well. This area was an important wine region during the Middle Ages, when monks from nearby monasteries used wines made here for Mass. Get more information at *www.conca.altanet.org*

Empordà

In the far northern corner of Catalonia, the DO Empordà has been a site of vineyards and winemaking since Greeks first settled here in 600 BC. Red and rosé wines made from grapes like Cariñena, Garnatxa and Tempranillo form the bulk of production here, though many international grape varieties are planted too. One of the most popular Empordà wines is Garnatxa Dulce, which is a sweet red wine made by traditional methods.

Vintage bottles of Catalan wines

Cabernet Sauvignon made in the Penedès

and to the large winery Torres, which introduced modern methods and international varieties to the region.

Traditionally a white wine region, Penedès is typically recognised for its cava, and for fruity whites. It has also gained a reputation for its equally fruity, well-balanced reds. Traditional grape varieties such as Garnatxa, Tempranillo and Macabeu are planted alongside international newcomers like Merlot, Chardonnay and Cabernet Sauvignon. See more at *www.dopenedes.es*

Montsant

A slate-filled region west of Tarragona, Montsant is a newly formed DO that's known for its strong red wines. Forming a ring around the Priorat region, Montsant has a lot in common with its more famous neighbour, and though new this region has a lot of potential. Already winemakers are following Priorat's example and are trying to make low-yield, high-quality wines, a strategy seen in the prices, which like Priorat's tend to be on the high side.

Penedès

Catalonia's best-known region, Penedès also has a long winemaking tradition, though it owes its modern reputation to the abundance of cava (sparkling wine) producers in the area

Priorat

One of Catalonia's top regions, Priorat is known for its intense, mineral-tinged red wines. Very few white wines are made here, as the poor slate soil and intense sun are better suited to red grapes like Garnatxa and Syrah. See *www.priorat.org*

Perfect grapes

Cycling is the best way to see the Delta

DELTA DE L'EBRE

With its wild, untamed coastline, empty beaches and fascinating bird life, the Ebro River Delta is a captivating area. A marshy wetland, this is one of Spain's most important natural reserves, and it welcomes tens of thousands of water fowl each year, with the population peaking in early autumn. This area is also an important centre of rice cultivation, and many highways run alongside watery rice fields.

Deltebre

This town is the gateway into the Ebro Delta Natural Park. A few hotels, restaurants and services make this a good base for exploring the park.

Ecomuseu

Visit this small museum for a close-up look at the environmental elements of the river delta. Examples of various delta habitats and the species that live in them make this a good place to learn about why this area is such an important natural reserve.
Carrer Doctor Martí Buera 22. Tel: 97 770 2954; www.museumontsia.org. Open: Mon–Fri 10am–2pm & 3–6pm, Sat 10am–1pm & 3.30–6pm, Sun 10am–1pm. Admission charge.

Parc Natural del Delta de l'Ebre

More than 10 per cent of all Iberian aquatic birds pass through the Ebro River Delta at some time of year. This

Southern Catalonia

immensely important natural habitat is home to more than 300 different species, and the park here protects this land and ensures that it will continue to be a suitable environment for the birds.

Some of the best spots for bird watching are the Laguna del Canal Vell (Lagoon of the Old Canal), where you'll see numerous wild ducks, the Isla de Sant Antoni (St Anthony's Island) and the mouth of the Ebro River, where you're guaranteed to see a variety of birds. This is a great area to tour in a boat, and numerous area companies offer short cruises here.

Information Centre and Ecomuseu del Delta. Carrer Martí Buera 22, Deltebre. Tel: 97 748 9679; www.ebre.com/delta

Beaches

The beaches of the Delta de l'Ebre can't boast seaside bars or rows of lounge chairs for rent, but they offer one of the most scenic sand-and-sea experiences

BIKING THE DELTA

With its flat terrain and stunning views, the Ebro Delta is simply made for cycling. One of the best routes takes you from Deltebre, into the Ebro Delta Natural Park and out to the Punta de Fangar, where there is a pretty lighthouse. Another route begins in La Cava and loops through the natural park. Get more information on routes and bike rental at *www.gencat.net/probert* or at the park information office.

in Catalonia. Wide stretches of pristine beaches run up and down the coast. Some of the best are the Platja de Ruimar and the Punta de Fangar, a peninsula where you'll see many bird species.

Sant Jaume d'Enveja

This town is a hub of sorts (albeit a modest one) for the area, and you'll probably have to pass through here, even if it's only to catch the ferry that shuttles cars and people from one side of the river to the other.

The Parc Natural's pristine coastline offers peace and solitude

The Costa Brava

Sitting just south of the French border, the Costa Brava ('brave' or 'rugged' coast) is perhaps the best-known area of Catalonia. Its rocky, cliff-lined coasts and the small coves they hide have drawn artists, travellers and sun-seekers ever since Spain began opening itself to tourism in the 1960s. But there is much more to La Costa Brava than sun and sand. Inland, medieval villages like Besalú and Peralada are open history books, with their old stone streets and monuments.

Near the shore historic towns like Pals make ideal places to combine culture and beach fun. Nature-lovers flock to this corner of Catalonia as well. Water sports abound along the coast, and there are countless trails to hike or bike.

GIRONA (GERONA)

Sitting on the banks of the Onyar River, Girona is a small city but one of Catalonia's economic and cultural landmarks. An important Roman town because of its position on the Via Augusta (*see p125*), Girona also became a wealthy medieval centre, with a large Jewish community and a solid base of artisans who created the city's architectural jewels.

Girona's historic quarter is one of the best lessons in Catalan history. The Roman walls form the town's backdrop, and from here you have a good view of

Girona's famous coloured houses line the River Onyar

The Costa Brava

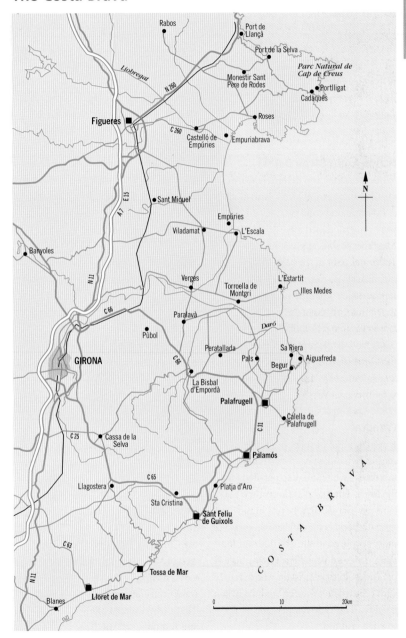

Rabos

Port de Llançà

Port de la Selva

Parc Natural de Cap de Creus

Llobregat

N 260

Monestir Sant Pere de Rodes

Portlligat

Cadaqués

Figueres

C 260

Roses

Castelló de Empúries

Empuriabrava

A 7 E 15

N

Sant Miquel

Empúries

Viladamat

L'Escala

Banyoles

N II

Verges

L'Estartit

Torroella de Montgri

Illes Medes

C 66

Paralavà

Daró

Pùbol

GIRONA

Peratallada

Sa Riera

C 86

Pals

Aiguafreda

Begur

La Bisbal d'Empordà

Palafrugell

C 25

Cassa de la Selva

C 31

Calella de Palafrugell

Palamós

C 65

Platja d'Aro

Llagostera

Sta Cristina

Sant Feliu de Guixols

C 63

C O S T A   B R A V A

N II

Tossa de Mar

Blanes

Lloret de Mar

0   10   20km

the medieval cathedral, the old Jewish *Call*, or quarter, beside it, and the modern city.

Tourist Office. Plaça de la Vila 1. Tel: 97 241 9010; www.ajuntament.gi or www.costabrava.org. Open: Sept–June Mon–Fri 9am–7pm, Sat 9am–2pm; July–Aug Mon–Fri 9am–3pm, Sat 9am–2pm.

Banys Arabs (Arab Baths)

While beautiful and definitely worth visiting, these really aren't Arab at all. A Romanesque construction, the baths were only modelled after those used by Muslims. The focal point here is the octagonal pool in the centre of an intimate stone room. The elegant Romanesque columns surrounding the bath are its most striking element.

Carrer Ferran el Catòlic. Tel. 97 221 3262; www.banyarabs.org. Open: Oct–Mar 10am–2pm; Apr–June & Sept 10am–7pm; July–Aug 10am–8pm. Admission charge.

Catedral

A combination of styles built over the centuries, Girona's cathedral is an impressive white building perched atop the town. The grand 18th-century baroque stairway that begins in the Plaça de la Catedral is the official entrance, but most people go in the side door off the Plaça de les Apóstols. The Gothic nave is the widest in the Christian world, at 23m (75ft). The towering vault truly is majestic. The 12th-century cloister is worth a visit too.

Museu de la Catedral (Cathedral Museum)

The highlight here is the Tapís de la Creació (Tapestry of the Creation), an 11th-century woven tapestry designed to hang behind the altar. The Beatus, an illustrated 10th-century book about the Apocalypse, is another treasure.

Plaça de la Catedral. Tel: 97 221 4426; www.lacatedraldegirona.com. Open: Oct–Feb 10am–2pm & 4–6pm; Mar–June 10am–2pm & 4–7pm; July–Sept 10am–8pm, closed Mon. Admission charge for Cathedral Museum.

Coloured houses

The colourful houses that line the River Onyar have become the symbol of Girona. The best place to get a view of them is from the various bridges that connect the new city with the old; the Pont de Pedra and Pont de Sant Agustí offer the best vantage points. What you're seeing are the backs of the houses that face the Carrer de les Ballesteries; these houses were built in the 17th century but have been modified and added to countless times through the centuries.

Església de Sant Feliu

Together with the cathedral's belltower, the Church of St Philip is the most recognisable object on Girona's skyline. Construction began in the 1300s but wasn't finished until 300 years later. That's why, as in so many churches and monuments, you'll see both

Romanesque and Gothic elements.
The oddly shaped belltower was
once topped by an intricate spire.
It was knocked clean off by a lightning
bolt, leaving the tower with an abrupt
flat top.
*Pujada de Sant Feliu 29. Open for
services only.*

La Lleona

In the Plaça de Sant Feliu you'll see
a skinny, rather ugly lion clutching a
stone column. This is Girona's lion, a
symbol of the city and the traditional
starting place for a stroll through the
centre. According to legend, if you kiss
the lion's hindquarters you'll be
able to return to the city some day in
the future.

Muralles Romanas (Roman Walls)

Girona's Roman defensive walls circle
around the back of the city, and the
path that runs atop them is the perfect
place to enjoy views of the city. The
wall path starts near the cathedral and
runs the length of the old city, ending
near Plaça Catalunya.
Open until dusk. Free admission.

Museu del Cinema

All right, so this museum has very little
to do with Girona or Catalan culture.
But it's a fun and fascinating look at the
history of cinema and animation.
There are artefacts, objects, drawings
and more going back nearly 500
years in search of the first traces of
moving pictures.

Girona

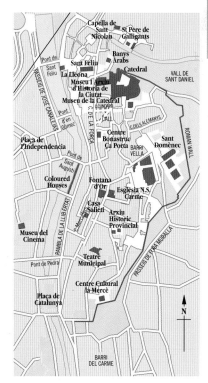

The Costa Brava

*Carrer Sèquia 1. Tel: 97 241 2777;
www.museudelcinema.org.
Open: Oct–Apr Mon–Fri 10am–6pm,
Sat 10am–8pm, Sun 11am–3pm;
May–Sept 10am–8pm.*

Museu d'Història de la Ciutat (City Historical Museum)

With interesting exhibits on life and
culture in Girona, this is a good place
to get a feel for the city's past.
*Carrer La Força 27. Tel: 97 222 2229;
www.ajuntament.gi/museu_ciutat.
Open: Tue–Sat 10am–2pm & 5–7pm.
Sun 10am–2pm. Admission charge.*

Jewish Girona

In the Middle Ages, Girona was home to one of Catalonia's largest Jewish communities. Jews began arriving in Girona from the Holy Land in the year 890, and for the next 600 years they lived, worked and worshipped here. Peace lasted until the Inquisition in the 15th century, when Spain's Catholic monarchs Ferdinand and Isabella expelled all Jews from the country, destroying the Jewish community in Girona and the rest of Spain. Though more than five centuries have gone by since then, countless remnants of Girona's medieval Jewish life are still visible in the old town.

The Mezuza

As you walk through the *Call*, or Jewish quarter, keep your eyes on the

The narrow streets and alleys of the old Jewish Quarter invite exploration

There is plenty of shade under the tall buildings

stone doorways of old buildings. On several door frames you'll see holes bored into the right-hand side at about shoulder height. These notches once held the *mezuza*, a tiny parchment bearing a few lines of scripture. The members of the household would touch the scriptures and say a short prayer every time they entered or left the house.

Carrer Força

The *Call*'s main street, Carrer Força was the centre of Jewish life from the 12th to the 15th century. The word *Call*, which is used to describe Jewish neighbourhoods all over Catalonia, means 'narrow' and refers to the set-up of the neighbourhood itself. The roads and alleyways here are certainly narrow; the thin, twisting streets are often no more than a metre (3ft) wide. These dark, often steep thoroughfares are what lend Girona's *Call* its romantic air.

Sant Lorenç and Carrer Cúndaro

To get a real feel for the labyrinth that was the medieval *Call*, head down the Callejón de Sant Lorenç and then back down Carrer Cúndaro. Other tunnel-like streets worth exploring include Escalinata del Quatre Cantons and Carrer Escola Pia.

SOUTHERN COSTA BRAVA

A fantastic variety of landscapes await in the southern stretch of La Costa Brava. Even though this area is most known for its seaside resorts, there are also a number of interesting cultural sites to explore.

Begur

This seaside village is special because of the 10th-century castle that crowns its shore. A lovely path leads up to the ruins, passing by four towers originally built to defend the town from pirates. From the castle's perch you have splendid panoramic views of the Costa Brava and the Illes Medes (*see below*) in the distance.
Tourist Office. Avinguda Onze de Septembre. Tel: 97 262 3479.

La Bisbal d'Empordà

This small inland town is known for one thing: ceramics. A stroll through the town centre will give you ample opportunity to admire the trademark jugs and plates of the area, often simple pieces glazed in just a few colours. This is a great place to pick up souvenirs, as the prices here tend to be the best you'll find anywhere in Catalonia.

Museu de la Terracota

Learn how La Bisbal's traditional ceramics are made at this small museum in the town centre. If you're into pottery, this will be a worthwhile stop.
Carrer 6 d'Octubre 99. Tel: 97 254 2067. Admission charge.

DIVING THE ILLES MEDES

On the Illes Medes there are dives for all styles. Beginners diving no more than 10m (40ft) deep will be able to spot lobsters and octopuses, while more experienced divers can head out to the rich coral landscapes that thrive in deeper, cooler waters.

Expert divers can explore the caves dug by time out of the rock massif. Caves like La Vaca (The Cow) feature a series of tunnels that house marine plants and fish. The mouth of La Vaca is well lit and ideal for photography, while its inner reaches are a mysteriously dark hole that guarantees a thrill.

There is even a wrecked ship nearby, which is one of the divers' favourite spots to explore. The *Reggio Messina*, intentionally sunk in 1991, is a short boat ride from the islands and is the largest diveable ship on the coast.

L'Estartit and Les Illes Medes

Just off the shore of the resort town of L'Estartit lie the Illes Medes, seven islets that are home to some of the most spectacular underwater scenery in the Mediterranean. As the natural habitat of some 1,350 species of marine life, the waters here rank as one of the top scuba diving spots in all Spain and are the unparalleled diving paradise of the Costa Brava. The area is so important that it has been declared a marine reserve and is strictly protected, with limits on the number of divers that can visit the site and a complete ban on fishing.

Geographically the islets form part of the Montgrí massif, a mountain-like rock formation that's the reason this stretch of coastline is so rugged. Over time, erosion carved out the irregular forms that we recognise today as the Illes Medes. The islets are scattered around the mouth of the organically rich River Ter, the source of a constant stream of food that nourishes lush marine plants and attracts dozens of marine species, including octopus, bream, lobster and starfish. Occasionally dolphins and big fish such as whale sharks and blue marlins appear as well.

La Estación Nautica. Carrer Platja 10–12. Tel: 97 275 0699; www.enestartit.com

Palafrugell

One of the largest towns on the coast, Palafrugell has long been an economic centre for the area and has an important cork industry. It's also known as the home of prolific Catalan writer Josep Pla, whose poems about Catalonia are some of the region's most important literary works. Many buses pass through Palafrugell, making this a common stop-over and a transport hub for this part of the Costa Brava.

Tourist Office. Plaça de l'Església. Tel: 97 30 0228; www.palafrugell.net

The Costa Brava

A secluded inlet on the southern Costa Brava

Tossa de Mar's old town and beaches

Calella de Palafrugell

A few kilometres from Palafrugell is the town's beach, Calella. One of the prettiest towns in the area, Calella has been an important fishing centre for centuries, and it still retains a sleepy, laid-back air (though you'll probably disagree with this assessment if you come in August). Several beaches run along the coast here; the Platja de Canadell is one of the prettiest. Countless *habaneras*, songs about seamen seeking their fortune in the New World, are sung about the fishermen from Calella.
Tourist Office. Carrer les Voltes 6. Tel: 97 261 4475.

Pals

Just inland you'll find the charming medieval town of Pals, one of the Costa Brava's most popular stops because of its ancient defence walls and old, twisted streets. Most of the interesting sights are huddled in the old quarter, the Barri de Sant Pere, a maze of streets built on a small hill. The Torre de les Hores de Pals (clocktower) is the main monument here.

Some 5km (3 miles) from the town centre is the Platja de Pals (Pals Beach), a popular seaside resort, with plenty of restaurants and hotels.

Peretallada

This is the kind of perfectly preserved medieval hamlet you thought existed only in the French countryside. Its stone, pedestrian-only streets still bear the ruts carved by the carts that once ran through, though few people actually live here now. The town is full of country inns and restaurants serving local Catalan dishes, but strolling the stone streets and admiring the 12th-century houses is a great option for a day trip. Staying in one of the intimate inns is also enjoyable, though take note that in the off-season Peretallada is nearly deserted and many establishments are closed.

Sant Feliu de Guíxols

One of the larger beach resorts, Sant Feliu de Guíxols is a pleasant place with a long seaside promenade and several wide beaches. The town was built up around the 10th-century Benedictine monastery of the same name, and now the monastery is one of the town's main sights. It is also known for its classical music festival, held annually in September.
Tourist Office. Plaça del Monestir 54. Tel: 97 282 0051; www.guixols.net

Tossa de Mar

Another busy resort, Tossa de Mar stands out for the ruins of its old town, which sit on a hill at the southern end of the shell-shaped beach. Modern apartments and hotels stretch out to the north and west, but the most interesting part of Tossa de Mar is the Vila Vella or old town, where you can follow a stone path up to the ruins of an old basilica, from which you can enjoy beautiful sea views. You can also walk atop the 12th-century defensive walls.

Just below the Vila Vella, the Vila Nova (new town) spreads out in a maze of narrow streets and quaint squares. Largely built in the 18th century, this area is now jam-packed with attractive restaurants and souvenir shops.
Tourist Office. Carretera de Lloret. Tel: 97 234 0108; www.infotossa.com

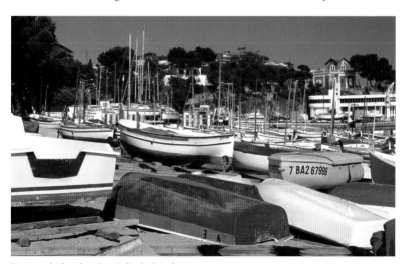

Boats on the beach at Sant Feliu de Guíxols

Coastal walk: Calella de Palafrugell to Llafranc

Trails run along many parts of La Costa Brava, providing an ideal way to enjoy the brilliant blue of the Mediterranean and the harsh rocky coast that provides such a beautiful contrast. This 2km (1¹/₄-mile), one-hour route (one-way) is one of the easiest and most representative stretch of coastal trail, but it's just an example of the many paths that run along the water.

1 Calella de Palafrugell

The trail begins at the northern end of Calella, at the Platja de Canadell (Canadell Beach). There is a car park nearby. Look out for the signpost pointing to the Camí de Ronda (Seaside Path) which is marked with a small coloured code indicated that you're on the GR-92, a massively long path that runs the length of Spain's Mediterranean coast and forms part of the E-10 route, which runs all the way to the Baltic.

2 Llafranc/Mediterranean views

The extremely easy-to-follow path runs along the shore. In many places you'll find a wooden rail guiding you along. Be sure to take a camera as this is one of the best areas to take photos of the coast and the town of Calella in the distance.

3 Plaça de Marinada

In about 30 minutes you'll reach the town of Palafrugell and its Plaça de Marinada. From here head to the Passeig de Cipsela, a pretty seaside

OF SMUGGLERS AND THIEVES

The pristine seaside trail you're about to take may seem like a simple path for sightseers and joggers, but it has a few dark secrets. In the past, these paths were popular ways for smugglers to move goods from boats inland, where they would be distributed via the smugglers' secret channels. These paths were also used by guards, who monitored ships coming in and out and tried to put a stop to the illegal activities in the area.

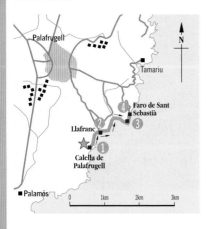

This coastal walk is well provided with viewpoints

promenade that follows the curve of Llafranc Bay. The promenade ends at the town's marina.

4 Faro de Sant Sebastià

From the marina, take the steps to your left (they're marked as the GR trail) and climb slowly to the Faro de Sant Sebastià (St Sebastian's Lighthouse). Along the way enjoy the fantastic views. In about 30 minutes you'll reach the lighthouse and a lookout point. Nearby you can also see the ruins of an old chapel and an Iberian settlement.

The Costa Brava's cliffs afford beautiful views of the Mediterranean

Bike tour: Vía Verde

Vías Verdes (Greenways, or Rail Trails) are fabulously straight, flat trails that follow abandoned railway lines. There are Vías Verdes throughout Spain and Catalonia, but this trail from Sant Feliu de Guíxols to Girona is one of the most scenic. Dubbed the Ruta del Carrilet (narrow-gauge railway route), it's ideal for biking, though you can walk stretches of it too.

Allow 3 hours for the 39km (24-mile) route by bike, one way.

For nearly 100 years the *Feliuet* train faithfully carried goods and passengers from the town of Girona to the important sea port of Sant Feliu, boosting the area's trade and improving communications within the region of La Selva. When bus services replaced the train in 1969, the railway line was abandoned and its 40km (25 miles) of track were left to rust.

As highways improved in the second half of the 20th century, this story was repeated all over Spain, resulting in the more than 7,000km (4,350 miles) of abandoned rails that criss-cross the country today. These trails were unused until 1993, when the Federación de los Ferrocarriles Españoles (FFE) started the *Vías Verdes* programme to convert the railway tracks into trails that could be enjoyed by bikers, walkers, horse riders and others. The trails, which follow the gentle slopes and easy curves of the tracks, are ideal for people with mobility problems, including those in wheelchairs. This 14-mile Girona–Costa Brava trail is no exception.

For more information about this and other greenways in Spain, check out www.viasverdes.com or call their office at 91 528 2815.

1 Sant Feliu de Guíxols

The easy-to-follow route begins in this seaside town (*see p103*), where you can see the ruins of a medieval monastery and enjoy fine views from the shore. The route begins in the upper part of Sant Feliu, about 1km (⅓ mile) from

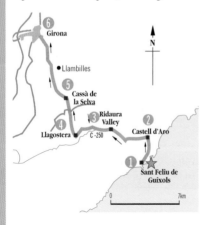

the beach. To reach the trail head, follow the Ronda de Joan Casas (just off the Rambla de la Generalitat), which converts into the old rail trail.

2 Castell d'Aro
The first interest point you come to, 4km (2¹/₂ miles) along the trail, is Castell d'Aro, a town with a hugely popular (and just plain huge) beach and a pretty but much-restored castle that gives the town its name. The town is visible from the trail but to visit it you have to make a small detour north.

3 Ridaura Valley
The packed-sand path continues on a (very) gentle incline through the Ridaura Valley, which strings between the Cadiretes massif and the Gavarres massif. This is a very smooth route.

4 Llagostera
After about 15km (9 miles) you'll reach the town of Llagostera, where you could take a detour to visit the ruined castle that sits on a hill at the top of the town.

5 Cassà de la Selva
In another 8km (5 miles) or so you'll reach Cassà de la Selva, a town known

Biking a *Vía Verde*

for its 'Parc Art', a natural park full of modern sculptures and outdoor artwork. More than three dozen Catalan, Spanish and international artists have works in the park.
Parc Art. Tel: 97 246 3081; www.parcart.net. Open: Apr–Sept Tue–Sat 10am–2pm & 4–8pm, Sun 10am–2pm; Oct–Mar Tue–Sat 10am–2pm & 4–6pm, Sun 10am–2pm. Admission charge.

6 Girona
The final 10–12km (6–7¹/₂ miles) of the route take you through the lovely Selva Depression, with its patchwork of cropland and forests, before leading you into the heart of Girona and the end of the route. If you wish, you can stay on this same trail all the way to Olot.

NORTHERN COSTA BRAVA

As you head towards the French border, the coast becomes ever more dramatic, providing a breathtaking backdrop for the exploration of ancient ruins, postcard-perfect villages and unspoilt natural spaces.

Cadaqués

It takes some effort to reach Cadaqués, a pristine fishing village that sits at the end of a long, winding road. Of course, that's probably why this idyllic spot has been able to withstand the onslaught of tourism and preserve its unique away-from-the-world feel. The whitewashed town is a tangle of narrow, cobblestone streets that make their way uphill to the Església de Santa María, whose simple belltower is the only thing marking the skyline of this low little village.

The main attractions here are the restaurants serving fresh Mediterranean fish, and the shore. Beaches are mostly pebbly and aren't ideal for swimming, but they couldn't be better for strolling. Fishing boats dot the protected bay that sits in front of town, creating a postcard-worthy view from shore. Also popular is the seaside path that curves around the bay and leads you to Portlligat, where Salvador Dalí once lived.
Tourist Office. Carrer Cotxe 2.
Tel: 97 225 8315.

Empúries

Empúries was first settled by the Greeks in 600 BC. Then called Emporion, which means 'market', it was indeed an important trading centre for the Greeks, thanks to its strategic location on the Mediterranean and near other Greek colonies.

By 100 BC the city had passed into Roman hands, and the Romans easily adapted the Greek foundations, building among and on top of the structures they found there. Yet when Emporiae, as the Romans called it, was raided by Germanic tribes in the late 5th century AD, it was finally abandoned. It wouldn't be discovered again until the 20th century, when archaeologists unearthed the remains of Catalonia's former first city.

Now you can visit the ruins of Emporion and Emporiae at the mostly outdoor Archaeological Museum here. These are ruins in the most basic sense of the word; expect to see the low foundations of houses, the outlines of roads and a few urban features, but little else. Though you may have to use your imagination to really grasp what the city would have looked like 1,600 years ago, this is nevertheless a fascinating place to explore and is one of Spain's most important archaeological sites.
Empúries–L'Escala. Tel: 97 277 0208;
www.mac.es. Open: June–Sept daily
10am–8pm; Oct–May 10am–6pm.
Admission charge.

Parc Natural de Cap de Creus

The Cap de Creus Nature Park stretches across nearly 14,000 hectares (34,600 acres) of northern Catalonia's shore, covering the dry, rocky hills and a large swathe of the Mediterranean itself, making it one of the few parks that protects both land and marine life. Hiking trails run throughout the park. *Information Office. Monestir de Sant Pere de Rodes. Tel: 97 219 3191; www.parcsdecatalunya.net*

Monestir de Sant Pere de Rodes

This Benedictine monastery inside the Nature Park has all the right elements for a romanticised journey through history: a mysterious and often violent past, a present structure evoking days of cloister gardens and pious meditation, and a pristine setting on Cap de Creus. Although it's been 200 years since the

monastery housed monks, the retreat's thousand-year history and quiet holiness still haunt the air.

A visit to the monastery is interesting in itself, but the mystery that surrounds it is more fascinating still. The monks who founded the Monestir believed that St Peter's skull and right arm were hidden in a cave somewhere on the mountain near the monastery, making the site holy. Through the centuries thousands of pilgrims have searched for them to no avail. The relics, along with many other bones, teeth and artefacts of the Catholic saints, were taken from Rome when the barbarians invaded the city in the 5th century. For protection, the

Ruins at Empúries include an early Christian basilica

relics were hidden in caves and forests throughout Europe and many, like St Peter's skull and arm bone, were never found.

The monastery has symbolic bones in a tomb inside, but some people still believe that the bones are on the mountain. Now only government-certified archaeologists can search the area, and most people regard the story as an unprovable legend.

Tel: 97 238 7559. Open: June–Sept Tue–Sun 10am–8pm; Oct–May Tue–Sun 10am–5.30pm. Admission charge.

Deserted, evocative Sant Pere de Rodes

This coastline is full of quiet coves and tiny beaches

Port de la Selva

Still an active fishing village, Port de la Selva sits on the coast just north of Sant Pere. There is not too much to see here, but the port is lined with fishing boats, and on workdays you can see the fishermen repairing nets, painting boats and bringing in the day's catch, making this an atmospheric place for a walk by the shore. The seafood restaurants here are especially good; be sure to ask for a locally caught fish.

Tourist Office. Carrer del Mar 1.
Tel: 97 238 7025.

Roses

Roses is one of the largest resort towns on the coast and sits on a wide bay that's served as a natural port for centuries. Though the modern part of town is basically a jungle of high-rise apartment buildings and cement pavements, you can also search out the attractive ruins of the city's citadel, built in the 16th century. The main wall is one of the few things left standing, but it serves to give a historic air to this bustling town. With plenty of accommodation options, good shopping and a lively nightlife, this is a popular holiday resort. Yet it's perhaps best known for being the home of chef Ferran Adrià's famous restaurant, El Bulli (*see next page*), which sits just outside town.

Tourist Office. Avinguda de Rhode 101.
Tel: 90 210 3636.

Ferran Adrià and Catalan cuisine

'Cooking is the only creative work, other than sex, that uses the four senses: sight, smell, touch and taste. Think about it; when you look at a work of art you don't usually taste it or smell it. But the sensations that cuisine can give you are incredible.'

Ferran Adrià

Newspapers from New York City to Tokyo have featured Catalan chef Ferran Adrià on their covers, and everyone who is anyone has fought for one of the few tables at his famed restaurant, El Bulli, near the northern Costa Brava resort of Roses. So what's the big deal about this self-made chef from Figueres?

Wildly innovative dishes like 'foams' – airy bits of nothing that he first discovered while blowing up tomatoes with a bicycle pump – and liquid raviolis that melt in your mouth have earned Adrià fans worldwide. His restaurant is considered to be the foodies' once-before-you-die experience, and it's nearly impossible to get a table.

Adrià has broken all the moulds of what food should look or feel like, earning him praise as 'the most creative chef in all history'. One of his most famous inventions is 'deconstruction', a process of separating the elements of certain dishes and recompiling them in new

Colourful food from El Bulli

Ferran Adrià in his kitchen

ways. He has pioneered the fusion of science and cuisine, starting a boom of gastronomic research and investigation that has drawn chefs from throughout Spain, Europe and beyond into its folds.

Adrià is at the forefront of creative cuisine in Spain, and his impact on the world food scene is undeniable. Yet he says that neither accolades nor fame drive him. 'I work to have a good time. I'm passionate about cooking, and I do exactly what I want,' he said.

In Adrià's case, doing what he wants means 'not copying' his past work or others, so every year he develops an all-new menu for El Bulli, closing the restaurant for six months and working with a team of chefs in a central Barcelona workshop to develop and perfect new techniques. Chefs work on things like 'centrifugation',

a way of separating the solid matter from liquids, and they practise quick-freezing foods. They burn rice, curdle milk, put slivers of dry ice inside food, all just to see what happens.

'For us, investigation is all about giving pleasure. Until now, not much work had been done to find out the "why" behind our food. But that's changing.'

Getting a table at El Bulli is difficult, but if you're able to do it, prepare for an unforgettable gastronomic experience.

To get an idea of Adrià's cooking, you can try one of his new, superior fast-food restaurants call Fast Good. *El Bulli. Tel: 972 150 457; email: bulli@elbulli.com. Open: Apr–Sept dinner only. Expect to pay around €200 per person.*
Fast Good. Calle Balmes 127, Barcelona. www.fast-good.com

DALILAND

The northwestern pocket of Catalonia has been dubbed 'Daliland' because it was the stamping ground of Surrealist artist Salvador Dalí. Following in the artist's footsteps is a popular pastime, and Figueres is a good starting point.

Figueres

Salvador Dalí was born here in 1904, and the main attraction in town is the museum he established to showcase his work. But this small city, located some 12km (7½ miles) inland, offers other interesting sights as well. Visit the Museu de Joguets (Toy Museum) to see Catalonia's largest collection of *caganers* (*see box*). At the Museu de l'Empordà (Empordà Museum) you'll learn more about the ancient and recent history of the whole region.

Museu de Joguets. Carrer Sant Pere 1. Tel: 97 250 4585; www.mjc-figueres.net. Open: June–Sept Mon–Sat 10am–1pm & 4–7pm, Sun 11am–1.30pm. Admission charge. Museu de l'Empordà. La Rambla 2. Tel: 97 250 2305; www.museuemporda.org. Open: Mon–Sat 11am–7pm. Admission charge.

Teatre-Museu Dalí

Designed by Dalí himself in 1974, this sprawling museum is a veritable temple to Surrealism. It's a sprawling space filled with Dalí's paintings, sculptures, sketches and installations from the artist's early days to the end of his life. Some of the most famous works include greats like *Soft Self-Portrait with*

THOSE CRAPPY CATALANS

The next time you see a Christmas manger scene in Catalunya, look closely at the figures inside. Mary, Joseph and baby Jesus are still the centre of the action, but there in the corner, behind the sheep and the bale of hay, you'll likely see a tiny red-capped figure squatting over a fresh pile of poo. The *caganer* or pooping man is an old, sacred tradition in Catalunya. He represents fertile soil and the cycle of life, and though he might seem offensive to the uninitiated, to the Catalans he is pure fun. *Caganers* are now made and sold in all kinds of guises – even in football strip – but the traditional type is always depicted wearing the *barretina* or red hat.

Fried Bacon (1941) and *The Spectre of Sex Appeal* (1932). Be sure to seek out the *Rainy Cadillac*, a bizarre sculpture using a real Cadillac whose interior is drenched with near-constant rain. Standing atop the car is a sculpture of Dalí's lover and muse, Gala. Nearby is the Mae West room, created especially for the museum. It features a series of abstract objects that, when viewed from a particular point, create the image of Mae West's face.

The museum was built atop the old Figueres theatre, which was destroyed during the Civil War.
Tel: 97 267 7500; www.dali-estate.org. Open: July–Sept Tue–Sun 9am–7.45pm; Oct–June Tue–Sun 10.30am–5.45pm. Admission charge.

Púbol

The medieval castle of Púbol was a gift from Dalí to Gala, who lived here in the 1970s. Dalí decorated the inside and the gardens, filling them with his own drawings, paintings and sculptures. Most interesting are the long-legged elephant sculptures in the yard. Dalí himself lived in the castle in the 1980s, after Gala died. He left the castle after it was damaged in a fire (a fire that put him in the hospital) in 1984.
Púbol, La Pera. Tel: 97 248 8655; www.salvador-dali.org. Open: mid-

Mar–mid-June 10.30am–6pm; mid-June–mid-Sept 10.30am–8pm; mid-Sept–early Jan 10.30am–6pm. Admission charge.

Portlligat

Dalí lived in this tiny fishing hamlet for much of his later life, and scenes from the shore here are seen in countless paintings. His house is now open to the public and is a great way to get an inside look at the artist's life. Full of Dalí's own furniture, books and knick-knacks, this sprawling Mediterranean retreat is a must-see for Dalí fans.
Portlligat. Tel: 97 225 1015; www.salvador-dali.org. Open: by reservation only, mid-Mar–mid-June 10.30am–6pm; mid-June–mid-Sept 10.30am–9pm; mid-Sept–early Jan 10.30am–6pm. Admission charge.

The Costa Brava

As extravagant as the man himself, the Dalí Museum in Figueres

Central Catalonia

This is the Catalan heartland, a traditional area where agriculture is still a major economic engine and Romanesque churches stand side by side with modern creations. Medieval towns, Romanesque monuments and pretty mountain settings mark the string of towns between Vic in the east and Lleida in the west.

Berga

With its origins going back to the ancient days of the Visigoths and Romans, Berga is an historic town tucked into the edge of the Pyrenees. The centre is easily walkable and is lined with pretty old houses, historic monuments and quiet squares, especially along the busy Carrer Major. Seek out the Església de Sant Joan (St John's Church), which has both Romanesque and Gothic elements.

Berga is worth touring any time of year, but it's best known for its wild summer fiesta, La Patum de Berga, held every year around the time of Corpus Christi (June). A fiery festival that can be shocking to visitors, the Patum features giant statues made of grass and straw that are set on fire in the middle of the crowded streets and squares. If you participate, wear all-cotton clothing and a hat that will protect you from sparks.

Tourist Office. Carrer Àngels 7.
Tel: 93 821 1384; www.ajberga.es

Cardona

Cardona's claim to fame is its huge Muntanya de Sal (Salt Mountain), a tremendous pile of, you guessed it, salt, which was mined here until 1990. These days it's a tourist attraction that draws in school groups and curious salt-lovers from Catalonia and beyond. Also worth visiting here is the fortified castle that towers above town. Peek in the Romanesque Església de Sant Vicenç (St Vincent's Church); its lovely frescoes have been moved for safekeeping to the Museu Nacional d'Art de Catalunya (*see p61*) but the church is beautiful just the same.

Muntanya de Sal. Carrer de la Mina.
Tel: 93 869 2475; www.salcardona.com.
Open: Tue–Fri 11.30am–1.30pm,
Sat–Sun 10am–2pm & 3.30–5pm.
Admission charge.

Lleida

The provincial capital and one of Catalonia's largest cities, Lleida (Lérida in Spanish) is a sprawling city that

stretches out along the scraggly Segre River. Though the modern city is not in the least bit enticing, the historic centre is worth a visit. Walk along the Carrer Major to see the Seu Nova (new cathedral), La Paeria (the town hall) and the Hospital de Santa María, which now houses an archaeological museum.
Tourist Office. Carrer Major 31.
Tel: 97 370 0319; http://turisme.paeria.es.
Archaeological Museum. Carrer Major.
Closed Mon. Admission charge.

The Old Cathedral in Lleida

La Seu Vella (Old Cathedral)

Lleida's most outstanding monument, this cathedral towers over the city centre, with a lovely Gothic belltower that's absolutely magical when illuminated at night. Built on top of a Muslim mosque, the cathedral was constructed in the early 13th century and was consecrated in 1278. The cloister and belltower were added later. The cathedral is in fine condition, surprisingly so given that it was used as a prison and stables for many years!

One of the most interesting elements of the cathedral are the fortified walls that surround it. The complex was built over seven centuries and wasn't completed until the 1800s. Now you can visit the *recinto* (complex) and walk among the historic walls.
Tel: 97 323 0653. Open Tue–Sun summer 9am–1.30pm & 4–7.30pm; winter 10am–1.30pm & 3–5.30pm.

Ripoll

Ripoll is famous as the legendary birthplace of Catalonia (it was the home of Wilfred the Hairy, *see pp14–15*) and for its Romanesque Basilica, Santa María del Ripoll (*see p130*).

Central Catalonia

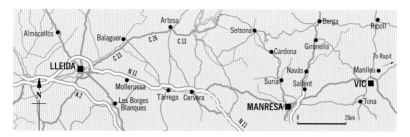

Central Catalonia

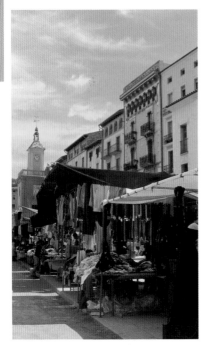

Part of Vic's extensive city market

Rupit

This tiny mountain town northeast of Vic sits on the edge of the Pyrenees and is one of the best preserved in the region. Strolling its narrow streets among old stone houses with flowering balconies is a joy. The traditional-style houses are the main draw here, but you can also visit the neoclassical Església de Sant Miquel (St Michael's Church) or the Capilla de Santa Magdalena (Chapel of St Mary Magdalene), which offers pretty views.

Solsona

A quaint town that's now an agricultural centre for the area,

Solsona is primarily known for its unique and rather disturbing tradition of hanging up donkeys (now only imitation ones are used) from the central belltower. Once you've had a good look at this belltower, also take a stroll to see the pretty Catedral de Santa María de Solsona, a hotchpotch of architectural styles including Romanesque, Gothic and baroque. Construction on the cathedral began in the 11th century and finished some 700 years later.
Tourist Office. Carretera Basella 1. Tel: 97 348 2310; www.elsolsonesinvita.com

Vic

The capital of Osona, Vic is an important cultural and economic centre for the region. Considered one of the most 'Catalan' towns of Catalonia, tradition-rich Vic is an interesting place for a one- or two-day stop, or to use as a base for excursions around central Catalonia.
Tourist Office. Carrer de la Ciutat 4. Tel: 93 886 2091; www.victurisme.ajvic.net

History

First an Iberian settlement, Vic later passed through the hands of the Romans and then the Visigoths. It was taken over by the Muslims but was later abandoned. Finally, Vic was officially re-founded and re-populated by Count Wilfred the Hairy (*see pp14–15*) in AD 878.

Plaça Major

The centre of the city is its famous Plaça Major, also called the Mercadal because it's the site of a city market. The market, held on Tuesdays and Saturdays, is a spectacle worth sticking around for. Farmers and artisans flock in from nearby towns to sell their delicious sausages, cheeses, honeys and fresh goods. The plaza itself, a sprawling arcaded square lined with colourful houses, is worth a visit on its own merit.

Catedral de Sant Pere

Vic's cathedral of St Peter is one of the most famous in Catalonia. What you see today is a combination of many styles, the result of countless additions and transformations through the years. Originally built in the 9th century under the orders of Wilfred the Hairy, it's now a largely neoclassical church. Yet you can still see the original Romanesque belltower, the 11th-century crypt and the Gothic cloister. The main building was designed by Josep Moretó in the late 18th century.

Catedral de Sant Pere. Plaça Catedral. Tel: 93 886 4449. Open 10am–1pm & 4–7pm.

Templo Romano

On the Plaça de la Pietat this Roman temple was only discovered in 1882, but it is a well-preserved (and largely rebuilt) temple complete with imposing columns at the entrance and a Rome-worthy peaked roof.

Central Catalonia is a land of fertile valleys and wooded hills

Tour: Medieval monasteries

This is one of the most dramatic historical and cultural routes Catalonia has to offer. The drive will take you through the low hills and vineyards of the comarcas Alt Camp, Conca de Barberà and Urgell as you visit perfectly preserved Cistercian monasteries and medieval towns where religious communities have lived for hundreds of years.

1 Santes Creus

The route begins just north of the A-2 motorway in the medieval enclave of Santes Creus, a town centred around the monastery of the same name. Founded in 1150, this monastery housed an active religious community for centuries, though it was abandoned in 1835 and is now strictly the domain of tourists. The delicate construction combines Romanesque and Gothic elements. Highlights of the visit include the splendid cloister and the royal apartments.

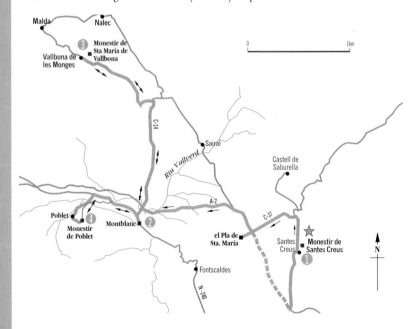

Tourist Office. Plaça Sant Bernat 1.
Tel: 97 763 8141; www.altcamp.
altanet.org. Monastery. Tel: 97 763 8329.
Open: mid-Mar–mid-Sept 10am–1.30pm
& 3–7pm, mid-Sept–mid-Jan 10am–
1.30pm & 3–5.30pm, mid-Jan–mid-Mar
10am–1.30pm & 3–6pm, no guided tours
Mon. Admission charge, Tue free.

2 Montblanc

Get back on the A-2 motorway heading towards Lleida, and take the exit marked 'Montblanc centre'. Montblanc's medieval centre is a magical place to stroll and soak up the atmosphere nine centuries of history have left here.

The old city walls, built in the 15th century, still surround much of the town. In the centre, visit the Església de Santa María, which boasts a lovely Renaissance portal. Climb to the top of the church belltower for a pretty view.

The town is most famous for its Setmana Medieval, a medieval festival in April with costumed merchants selling in old-time markets and activities based on medieval traditions.
Tourist Office. Antiga Església de Sant Francesc. Tel: 97 786 1733;
www.montblancmedieval.org

3 Vallbona de les Monges

Now head north on the C-14 highway. Some 5km (3 miles) past Solivella turn left on a small local highway to reach the Monasterio de Santa María de Vallbona de les Monges. The most important female Cistercian house in Catalonia. Guided visits (usually in Catalan) lead you through the Romanesque cloister and to the lovely but bare church, which has elements of both Romanesque and Gothic styles.
Tel: 97 333 0266; www.vallbona.com.
Open: Nov–Feb 10am–1pm &
4.30–7pm, Sun 12–1.30pm & 4.30–7pm.
Admission charge.

4 Poblet

Take the C-14 again, this time headed south. When the highway meets up with the N-240 turn right and follow the signs to Poblet.

This is the largest inhabited Cistercian monastery in Europe (with a community of 70 or so) and monks have been living here since 1153. One of the best-loved and best-known monasteries in Catalonia, Poblet has a privileged setting among rolling vineyards and boasts splendid architecture. The fortified walls surrounding it add to the beauty.

Inside, you can tour the peaceful cloister, the main church and Panteón de los Reyes (the Royal Pantheon, where many kings of Aragón and Catalonia are buried). You'll also get to walk through the inner area of the monastery to see the library, a monk's cell and the old wine cellar.
Tel: 97 787 1247 or 97 787 0254;
www.concadebarbera.info. Open: mid-
Oct–mid-Mar Mon–Sat 10am–12.45pm
& 3–5.30pm, Sun 10am–12.30pm &
3–5.30pm; mid-Mar–mid-Oct Mon–Sat
10am–12.45pm & 3–6pm, Sun 10am–
12.30pm & 3–5.30pm. Admission charge.

The Pyrenees and Pre-Pyrenees

The Catalan Pyrenees don't fit the stereotypical image of Spain. A far cry from the sun-and-sand of the coast, the Pyrenees are a lush green land seemingly better suited to central Europe than to sunny Spain. With jagged rock peaks and pretty green valleys, the Pyrenees and the lower hills of the Pre-Pyrenees offer outstanding scenery and plenty of options for lovers of the outdoors.

LA GARROTXA

Garrotxa is the 'land of volcanoes', a hilly green region where ancient volcanoes lie. Though there have been no eruptions here for thousands of years, the volcanoes are technically still active. Nature is the major draw here but nearby you'll also find the pretty medieval town of Besalú and the legend-laden Banyoles.

Banyoles

In Banyoles, Catalonia has its very own Loch Ness. The small lake here, today used for recreational boating, is the source of countless legends. The most famous one claims that a monster lives at the bottom of the lagoon, though the cynical say that 'legend' was invented in the 20th century to boost the budding tourist industry around the lake. Monsters or no, this is a pretty place to enjoy an easy boat cruise or canoe outing.
Tourist Office. Passeig Indústria 25. Tel: 97 257 5573; www.banyolesturisme.com

Besalú

Sitting beside the Fluvià River, pretty Besalú with its arcaded streets and squares is full of modern life and activity and is much more than an outdoor museum.

The highlight of Besalú (and its most-photographed sight) is the 11th-century stone bridge that spans the river. This fortified bridge is unusual because of the picturesque bend in its centre which allowed the bridge's foundation to be laid on the river rocks. An impressive crenellated gateway stands at its midpoint.

In town you can visit the Església de Sant Vicenç (St Vincent's Church, open for services only), a lovely Romanesque church founded in 977, though the belltower is from the 16th century. Also seek out the imposing Església de Sant Pere (St Peter's), one of the most important Romanesque churches in Catalonia. Today it sits on the large Prat de Sant Pere, a square that once served as the town's cemetery.

Besalú had an important Jewish population in the Middle Ages, and the Miqvé, or ritual bath, is one of its most interesting sights. Discovered by accident in the 1940s, this bath was used for ritual cleansings and as part of some special religious services. The ruins of a wall from the former synagogue stand near the Miqvé's entrance.

Tourist Office. Plaça Llibertat 1. Tel: 97 259 1240; www.ajuntamentbesalu.org. Miqvé. Open: Mon–Fri 10.30am, noon & 4.30pm, Sat–Sun also open 1.30pm & 6pm. Admission charge. Get tickets in tourist office.

Castellfollit de la Roca

The main draw of this tiny town is the view you get of it from the N-260 highway that runs between Girona and Olot. Perched on the edge of a vertical

Medieval Besalú seen from the bridge

rock cliff, the houses of Castellfollit de la Roca are pushed right up to the edge, looking as though they could tumble down at any moment. Since they haven't fallen since being built hundreds of years ago it's doubtful that they'll be going anywhere any time soon. Still, the sight makes you catch your breath.

Olot

Capital of the *comarca* or county, Olot has a charming centre with pedestrian-only shopping streets and a massive baroque church dominating them. The town is well laid out, largely owing to the two volcanoes that flattened the original city in the 15th century. Its easy-to-navigate streets were planned as part of the rebuilding after the disasters.

Most of what's truly interesting here lies outside town, in the volcanic nature park (*see p124*). To learn more about the park, the flora and fauna in it, and the volcanic landscape, visit the Casal dels Volcans, a volcano museum and botanical garden in Olot. Also in Olot itself you can see a few Modernist buildings in the centre and can visit the Museu Comarcal (County Museum), which boasts a large collection of Modernist paintings.

Casal dels Volcans. Avinguda Santa Coloma 43. Tel: 97 227 2777; www.olot.org/cultura. Open: Mon–Sat 10am–2pm & 4–6pm, Sun 10am–2pm. Tourist Office. Carrer Hospici 8. Tel: 97 226 0141; www.olot.org/turisme

Castellfollit de la Roca is one of the smallest municipal districts in Catalonia

Open: Mon–Sat 10am–2pm & 3–7pm, Sun 11am–2pm. Museu Comarcal. Carrer Hospici 8. Tel: 97 227 9130. Open: Wed–Sat & Mon 10am–2pm & 4–7pm, Sun 10am–2pm.

Parc Natural de la Zona Volcánica de La Garrotxa

In the Nature Park of the Garrotxa Volcanic Zone, bright green hillsides, pristine forests and medieval architecture create an atmosphere that's two parts fairy tale and one part historical journey. The stars of this varied landscape are undoubtedly the nearly 40 small volcanoes dotting the area. Most of the volcanoes are little more than green bumps on the face of the land. A few, like the volcano of the Croscat, show their dark interiors, from which bits of the almost weightless, pitted volcanic rock tumble in waves of grey, black and deep red.

These are no mile-high, snow-capped peaks, and most of the lava flow has long since been covered by plants eager to wiggle their roots into the fertile volcanic soil. The volcanoes have been inactive for more than 11,500 years, but the effects of their ancient eruptions have determined the lie of the land and the mix of plants and animals living there today.

For a good introduction to the park, visit the volcano museum in Olot.

Vía Augusta walk

For more than two millennia, the Via del Capsacosta (part of the Roman Via Augusta) was the main connection between the Pyrenees and the northern Catalan coast. Built some 200 years before Christ, it was a sturdy, stone-paved road that cut through the flatlands and wound around mountains. The road, which probably followed the path of an even older thoroughfare used by nomads or even animals, connected remote towns and allowed commerce to filter into the mountains.

Now an 8km (5-mile) section of it, between Sant Pau de Segúries in El Ripollès and La Garrotxa's Vall de Bianya, has been partially restored, making for a unique historical hike. One of the most interesting aspects of this ancient road is the abundance of modern-looking technical features, like trenches that allowed water to pass and safety barriers that prevented travellers from sliding off down the mountain.

The lush foothills of the Pyrenees seem more alpine than Mediterranean

The Pyrenees and Pre-Pyrenees

The Pyrenees region

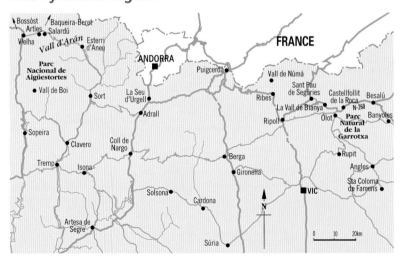

Walk: La Garrotxa

There are several well-marked walks that explore the centre of the Parc Natural de la Zona Volcánica de la Garrotxa, and this is an especially good one. It explores a peaceful beech forest then continues in a hike of medium difficulty up the Volcán de Santa Margarita, where a small chapel sits in the ancient crater. Finally, the trail heads past the Volcán del Croscat and back to the visitor's centre where it began.

Allow four hours.

1 Fageda d'en Jordà (Jordà Beechwood)

Begin your walk by the Area de Can Serra visitor's centre near the Fageda d'en Jordà, a forest immortalised by the Catalan Modernist poet Joan Maragall (1860–1911). A well-marked trail meanders through the forest and over the large volcanic rocks that threaten to trip anyone who takes a lingering look at the treetops. An irresistibly romantic air is created by the elegant beeches, the fresh woody smell and the occasional scampering of forest creatures.

2 Pla de Sacot

From here the trail climbs up the slope of Santa Margarita, a small cone-shaped volcano. The trail meanders over rocks and gets downright difficult for about 20 minutes, with a steep incline and a narrow walking space. You'll get some relief when you pass through the flat Pla de Sacot, a green valley carefully cultivated and cared for.

3 Santa Margarita

Santa Margarita is known for her perfectly shaped crater, a circle 350m (380yds) in diameter. Once the trail reaches the top of the mountain, it skirts the crater. The sides of the mountain, right up to the lip of the crater, are full of pines, oaks and various shrubs and plants. But the crater itself is barren inside. A little bit of brown grass pads the prairie, and a few dead-looking bushes creep up the sides. It could be the site of a UFO landing.

4 Capilla de Santa Margarita

The most interesting thing about the crater, other than the knowledge that you are quietly standing in what was once a pit that led to the fiery centre of the Earth, is the small stone chapel that sits in the middle of it. It's the perfect backdrop for a picnic.

5 Croscat

Now the trail heads towards the volcano of the Croscat, the largest volcano on the Iberian peninsula. Like Santa Margarita and the area's other volcanoes, Croscat was formed by a series of eruptions that left layers of lava, ash and minerals slowly building into a cone, or in Croscat's case, a horseshoe shape.

Unfortunately, one of the most interesting parts of the volcano of the Croscat is a result of irresponsible mining. A 500-m- (550-yd-) wide gorge

The sunlit beechwood of Jordà

has been cut into the side of the volcano by a mining explosion. The cut is fascinating, however, as it acts as a cross-section and shows the evolution of the volcano in layers of coloured rock. The rock dissolves into tiny pebbles, each like a fossil of a sponge, that slide away from the slope into dunes.

From here the trail makes its way back to the visitor's centre.

You can take a fascinating walk around Croscat Volcano

LA CERDANYA, VALL DE NÚRIA AND ENVIRONS

Surrounded by the peaks of the Pyrenees and full of lush, green vegetation, the valleys of La Cerdanya and Núria are pristine natural areas perfect for hiking or exploring by car.

La Seu d'Urgell

This is a frontier town of sorts, the last Spanish town you'll come to before entering into the neighbouring country of Andorra. This is one of the largest and economically most important towns in the Pyrenees, and historically it has been a powerful religious and administrative centre. These days it is known for its Parador hotel and quaint historic centre. The lovely Catedral de Santa María is definitely worth seeking out. Pay special attention to the ornate carvings on the cloister's columns. An illustration of Urgell's historic importance is that the Bishop of Urgell is one of the two nominal overlords of the state of Andorra (the other being the President of the French Republic as successor of the Kings of France).

Puigcerdá

The capital of La Baix (lower) Cerdanya, modern Puigcerdá is a prosperous town known for its textile industry and for its role as the region's tourism centre. Offering good shopping and great restaurant options, Puigcerdá is a popular base town for those wanting to explore the rest of

A typical village in La Cerdanya

Cerdanya and for skiers who come to try out the many slopes nearby.

Cerdanya once formed part of French Cerdagne (the two were split by a peace treaty in 1659, see p13) and the region still has many cultural ties with its neighbour. Expect to hear a bit of French and to see plenty of visitors from across the border, which is just a few kilometres away.
Tourist Office. Carrer Querol 1.
Tel: 97 214 0665.

Sort

A centre for adventure sports, Sort is the place to come if you're into white-water rafting, hang-gliding, rock climbing or quad biking. Thanks to the town's proximity to rivers and mountains, numerous outfitters have set up here. The town, whose name translates as 'Lucky', is also known for its lottery tickets. Hopefuls come in swarms to buy lucky tickets, and there have been several big winners in recent years.

Tourist Office. Carrer del Mig 9.
Tel: 97 362 1002;
www.noguerapallaresa.com

Vall de Núria

Long a point of pilgrimage for the faithful, the Vall de Núria is home to the Sanctuari de la Mare de Déu de Núria (Sanctuary of the Mother of God at Núria), a huge religious complex that dominates one end of the valley. Though the Sanctuari has given Núria her fame, the real attraction here is nature. An unspoilt mountain valley, Núria has been able to accept tourists without becoming encumbered with the traditional trappings of tourism. Cars are prohibited in the valley, and the only means of entry are walking in or riding the *cremallera*, a narrow-gauge railway that chugs its way up the mountainside and down into the valley. A ski resort was set up here in the 1930s, and you can still ski its slopes in winter. The seven runs are scenic but relatively simple runs and are perfect for families.

Tel: 97 273 2020; www.valldenuria.com

POT HEADS

The pilgrims who visit the Sanctuari de la Mare de Déu de Núria must do one thing before they leave: search out the pot and the bell. Tradition says that if you put your head in the pot and ring the bell (at the same time) women will be guaranteed fertility; the number of times they ring the bell is the number of children they'll have. Men doing the same guard themselves from headaches. One supposes that the men are guarding themselves against the headaches their future children will surely bring.

The snow-capped Pyrenees form a natural frontier between Spain and France

Catalan Romanesque

More than 2,000 Romanesque churches, houses and bridges are dotted about Catalonia's countryside, making this area one of Europe's best for appreciating and experiencing Romanesque art and architecture.

In the 11th century Catalonia was just coming into its own as an independent land, and the effort to unify and pacify it included founding churches and monasteries throughout the region. The Catalonia of those days, dubbed 'Old Catalonia' by modern historians, included much of the Pyrenees and Pre-Pyrenees. So it isn't surprising that that is where many of the Romanesque monuments are to be found.

The first medieval artistic movement that spread throughout Western Europe, Romanesque work can be seen from the British Isles down to southern Iberia. The works here in Catalonia are exceptional for their sheer number and for the excellent condition of many of them. Romanesque constructions are sturdy yet delicate, a perfect fit for the natural surroundings where they're often found. Common elements include semi-circular apses, narrow windows separated by pillars, arched doorways and square belltowers. These design elements appear over and over again in churches, monasteries and country manor houses.

Romanesque art developed after the style was established in architecture. Though to our modern eyes the flat drawings, with their

Part of a decorative arch at Santa María de Ripoll

A Romanesque rounded archway

decorative arch and seven horizontal bands packed with sculptures and decoration. The sculptures on the arch depict the months of the year and the rural activities that accompany the months. The bands stretching out to either side give the impression of being stone film, with every frame a scene that represents stories from the Bible or teaches a lesson in morality. Inside the Basilica is a beautiful cloister, with one elaborately decorated side.

elongated features and black outlines, look cartoonish, this style was sophisticated for the day. Unfortunately many Romanesque works have been removed from the buildings they were created for. Today museums like Barcelona's Museu Nacional d'Art de Catalunya (see p61) keep them safe and sound.

Santa María de Ripoll

Ripoll's Benedictine monastery, Santa María, is Catalonia's most famous example of the Romanesque. Founded in 879 by Catalonia's founder, Count Guifre el Pelòs (Wilfred the Hairy, see pp14–15), the monastery was added to over the years, the most famous addition being the fabulous 12th-century Romanesque doorway. Imposing wooden doors are surrounded by a

Basílica de Sant Viçenç de Cardona

Another masterpiece of the Catalan Romanesque, the majestic St Vincent's Basilica towers over Cardona (see p116) from its perch on a grassy hill. Built in 1040, the Basilica is in the shape of a cross, with a wide central nave and two additional aisles. For more on the Romanesque in Catalonia, see the Medieval Monasteries tour, pp120–21.

A typical semi-circular apse

Estany de Sant Maurici lies in the eastern part of the Parc Nacional de Aigüestortes

THE UPPER PYRENEES

The snow-capped tips of Spain's northernmost Pyrenees are a truly majestic sight. This is a hotspot for skiing in winter, when the valleys crowd with snow enthusiasts from Barcelona and Madrid. In spring and summer it's a paradise for hikers and bikers, who love having the valleys and peaks to themselves. With dozens of mountain lakes, kilometres of 4 × 4 trails and enough mountain peaks to keep you hiking for the rest of your life, the Pyrenees won't disappoint the active visitor.

Parc Nacional de Aigüestortes i Estany de Sant Maurici

Aigüestortes means 'twisted waters' in Catalan, and it's a fitting name for this national park, which is laced with meandering streams, wandering trickles and mountain torrents that give the whole place a fresh, wet feel. Nearly 41,000 hectares (101,000 acres) of mountain scenery are enclosed within its borders, marking what many people consider to be Catalonia's most breathtaking landscape.

You can't drive through the park, but numerous trails lead you past its glacial lakes, rivers and mountainsides. No camping is allowed within its borders, but there are several mountain refuges where you can eat or sleep (with a reservation). Some of the best-known sights include the Estany de Sant Maurici, a kilometre- (¹/₃ mile-) long lake, and the peaks of Els Encants that rise above it.
Tel: 97 362 4036; www. parcsdecatalunya.net/aiguestortes.htm

Vall d'Aran

The only north-facing valley in the Pyrenees, the Vall d'Aran has a distinctly French feel, due to the fact that it's much easier to get here from France than it is from the rest of Spain. In fact, this valley was pretty much disconnected from the rest of the Iberian peninsula until the 1950s, when a tunnel was dug through the mountain, finally obliterating the long mountain overpass that was once the only way to get from the Vall d'Aran to the rest of the country. The tunnel also allowed visitors in, paving the way for the skiing industry and accompanying tourism that is now the valley's mainstay.

There are literally hundreds of options for walking or hiking in the valley, including some long-distance routes that can last days. Your best bet is to buy a good walking guide and a detailed map. The tourist office

ARE YOU A 'SKY RUNNER'?

Of the countless trails in Aigüestortes, perhaps the most famous is the Carros de Foc (Chariots of Fire) trail, a challenging route covering nearly the entire park that usually takes five or six days to complete. The 60-km (37-mile) trail (which has a total altitude change of 9km/5.7 miles) passes spectacular scenery, but it's best known for the 'sky runners' who attempt to complete it in under 24 hours. The current record is just over 10 hours. Think you can beat that?
www.carrosdefoc.com

has some material, but their walking guides (available in English) leave much to be desired.
Tourist Office. Carrer Sarriulera 10. Tel: 97 364 0110; www.aran.org

Artíes and Salardú

Artíes and Salardú are neighbouring towns in the eastern end of the valley.

The Pyrenees and Pre-Pyrenees

The Vall d'Aran, once almost cut off from the rest of Spain

The Church of the Assumption, Bossòst

Artíes is the bigger of the two, with some of the valley's best restaurant and nightlife options (nightlife being defined as the town's three late-night bars). Both have attractive medieval churches and pretty squares to wander in.

Baqueira-Beret

Recognised as one of the best ski resorts in Spain, this is where the Spanish royal family and their entourage come to show off their skills on the slope. With a myriad of runs for all levels and tastes, this resort can almost (but not quite) compete with those of the French or Swiss Alps. Still, it is a well-kept and fairly priced place, and the scenery from the top is simply marvellous.

Baqueira-Beret. Tel: 97 363 9010;
www.baqueira.es

Bossòst

The last Spanish resort before you reach the French border, this quaint, tree-lined village is a pretty place for strolling or window shopping. A river rushes by on the edge of town, while in the centre the pretty Romanesque Església de l'Assumpció de María (Church of the Assumption) makes for a nice stop.

Vielha

The largest town in the Vall d'Aran, Vielha is the commercial and bureaucratic centre of the valley. The highway running through the middle of town is one long strip of outdoors shops and outfitters, with a few so-so bars and services like pharmacies and bookshops thrown in. Vielha is home to the area's only cinema and to a discotheque, as well as an ice-skating rink, all of which offer alternative activities on a stormy day. In summer, you'll find a half-dozen companies offering horse riding, quad bike excursions and adventure sports.

Vall de Boi

This hidden valley has some of Catalonia's most beautiful Romanesque churches and is a fantastic place to explore by car. Head to Taüll to marvel at Sant Climent de Taüll (St Clement's), a soothingly elegant church considered one of Catalonia's best examples of the Romanesque style. Also here in town is Santa María de Taüll, another Romanesque gem. Both have irregular opening hours.

This valley is also the home of Caldes de Boi, a large health spa based on the healing powers of the waters here. The spa, which makes a relaxing base for hiking in the area, offers treatments ranging from mud masks and massages to anti-stress and weight-loss programmes. There has been a guesthouse on this site since 1671, and the place seems as popular as ever. *Caldes de Boi. Tel: 97 369 4000.*

SPEAK ARANÉS

The Pyrenean Vall d'Aran was so isolated for so many generations that it developed its own language (usually considered a dialect of Catalan) called Aranés. The language, which sounds a lot like Catalan, has fallen into disuse, but it's now being taught again in schools and is used by the Aranése local government.

Basic Aranés:

Yes: Òc

No: Non

Goodbye: Adishatz

Party: Hèsta

Mountain refuges in the Pyrenees offer accommodation and food to walkers

Walk: Vall d'Aran

This easy-to-medium-difficulty walk begins in the Pla de Beret and leads you around green hills and in the shadow of majestic mountains to reach the abandoned town and sanctuary of Montgarri, today a refugio *where you can get lunch or a snack. The 12km (7¹/₂-mile) circular route is best walked between June and October, when there is no snow to bury the trail.*

Allow four hours.

1 Pla de Beret
The flat 'Plain of Beret' is the starting point for the journey. Park in the large car park here, then look for the path in the far northern (left) corner. This is a part of the longer GR-211 trail, and though it begins as an ill-defined path across a muddy prairie, it soon becomes a stable earth trail.

2 Riu de Barlongueta
You'll cross the narrow Barlongueta River (just wade it!) after 1.7 km (1 mile). Soon after, you enter into a small, shady pine forest. In 1.3km (³/₄ mile) you'll cross another small river (though depending on the time of year it may be a mere trickle), the Riu de Parros. Cross it and continue on, across a meadow and down into a little gully.

3 Pont de Cabau and Es de Cabau
Once you cross this small cement bridge (at about the km 4/mile 2¹/₂ of the walk) you'll know you're nearing

the sanctuary. Begin the steepish climb up to the thatched house, Es de Cabau. Here the GR-211 trail branches off to the left, but you should stay straight towards Montgarri, which will soon come into view.

4 Montgarri
At 5.4 km (3¹/₃ miles) from the start of the walk after walking downhill through a small hazelnut grove and beside a large field, you'll reach the

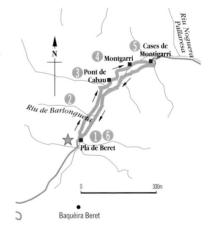

The flat part of the Vall d'Aran is an easy walk …

door of Montgarri. Here you can visit the ruined church or stop for a snack in the refuge here.

5 Riu Noguera Pallaresa and Cases de Montgarri

As you leave Montgarri you'll cross the Noguera Pallaresa River; turn left. The path continues, descending as it passes a group of abandoned houses (the Cases de Montgarri), a vestige of the days when this was a small, agricultural community.

6 Return to Pla de Beret

At 6.6km (4 miles) from the start, head southwest (right), climbing through a pine forest on a wide track. From here, the 6km (3³/₄ miles) back to the starting point is straightforward and very easy

to follow, much of it following the track used by vehicles. You'll have to cross a few straggly rivers and be back at the car park in well under two hours.

… and for the forest trails of Aran, waterproof footwear is advisable in spring and autumn

Getting away from it all

If you want to escape the crowds, try a new activity or delve deeper into Catalan culture, there are a myriad of options waiting beyond the hustle and bustle of the more traditional tourist attractions. What follows are just a few suggestions of alternative activities.

Adventure and extreme sports

Alta Ruta

Canyoning, a sport where you descend rivers by swimming, floating, leaping or rappelling them, is quickly gaining popularity in Spain. This company offers a variety of opportunities for beginners or skilled canyoners.
Sort. Tel: 97 362 6513;
www.altaruta.com.
Excursions approx. €25–50.

Centre de Paracaigudisme (Sky Diving Centre)

Even novices can sky dive. Jumpers tandem dive with a professional from an aeroplane flying nearly 4,000m (13,000ft) high. This is definitely a memorable way to see Catalonia.
Empuriabrava, Costa Brava. Tel: 97 245 0111; www.skydiveempuriabrava.com.
Jump from approx. €140.

Cicloturisme

Cicloturisme organises personalised group or solo cycling tours in Catalonia. Cicloturisme can also carry your luggage or advise you about routes. Day trips and long-term trips are available.
Carrer Santa Clara, Girona.
Tel: 97 222 1047; www.cicloturisme.com.
Trips from approx. €30/day.

Collectiu Natrix

Offering all kinds of adventures ranging from canoeing to mountain climbing, this Valls-based company leads excursions, provides equipment and advises about safety.
Valls. Tel: 97 761 3224.
Activities from approx. €18/day.

Parapent Passió

Something between hang-gliding and flying, parapenting is a thrilling way to see the Catalan landscape. An experienced flyer will accompany you on a 600m (2,000ft) ride down from a mountain peak.
Tel: 609 853 224;
www.parapent-passio.com

Quad Priorat

Take in the beauty of the Priorat region from your perch on a rough-and-ready quad biking ride.

Tel: 97 782 5243; www.priorat.org. From approx. €35/hour.

Rubber River

Go white-water rafting, canoeing, kayaking or canyoning on the Noguera Pallaresa River in the Pre-Pyrenees. The best time to go down the river is in late spring, when the melted snow from the mountains ensures a rushing river. The company also offers horse riding, hot-air balloon rides, paragliding and more.

Sort. Tel: 97 362 0220; www.rubberriver.com. Activities from approx. €20.

Cultural activities

Astronomy nights on Collserola

Barcelona's Collserola mountain range is the site for weekly astronomy nights, when park scientists talk to you about the stars and planets visible from here.

Consorci del Par de Collserola. Tel: 93 280 3552. Admission approx. €4.

Catacurian

Catacurian offers week-long culinary holidays in Catalonia's Priorat region. Focus is on learning about area wines, traditional Catalan dishes and local agriculture. In season, the holiday includes helping with olive or grape harvests or hunting for wild mushrooms.

Masroig, Priorat. Tel: 93 511 0738

Getting away from it all

Learning about Catalan cuisine at Catacurian

Olive-picking near Tarragona is one of the region's numerous activities available

(English spoken); www.catacurian.com; email: info@catacurian.com. One week from approx. €2,000.

Fundació Castells Culturals

If you like castles you'll love the tours arranged by the Cultural Castles Foundation in Lleida. Guided tours are given of historic castles throughout the region. You can choose to visit just one castle or to create a longer itinerary of Catalan castles.
Noguera, Lleida. Tel: 97 340 2045; www.castellscatalunya.com. Castle visit approx. €5.

GR Sports – olive preparation

Olives are a big part of Catalonia's economy and food culture. Learn how to harvest and prepare them at this unique centre near Tarragona.
Montsià, Tarragona. Tel: 630 126 953. From approx. €25/day.

Golf
Mas Pagès Golf

A lovely course set by a pristine forest, this is an entertaining if not very challenging course, which is good for beginner and intermediate golfers. Classes are available to book.

Carretera L'Escala–Banyoles.
Tel: 97 256 1001; www.maspages.org.
18 holes approx. €10–15.

Riding
Hípica Els 4 Vents
There's no better way to soak up the beauty of the rural Conca de Barberá than from your perch on the back of a horse. Guided excursions, horse hire and courses available.
L'Espluga de Francolí. Tel: 97 787 0619. Approx. €15/hour.

Sea fishing
Centre de Pesca Esportiva
Fish the Mediterranean as you enjoy the soothing seascape of the Delta de l'Ebre. All fishing equipment is provided.
Deltebre. Tel: 97 748 9231; www.ebrodeltagarbi.com. Excursions from approx. €40 per day.

Costa Brava fishing
Head out for some deep sea fishing on the Mediterranean. With sleek boats and the most sophisticated equipment, Costa Brava Fishing practically guarantees a catch.
Calle Sant Josep Oriol, Figueres. Tel: 610 556 699. Approx. €500 per group per day.

Water sports and sailing
Catavent
Renting out windsurfs, catamarans and kayaks, Catavent offers many ways to experience the Mediterranean. Courses are also available.
Arenales del Mar, Pals. Tel: 97 261 2248. Prices vary.

Costa Mágica
Sail along the Costa Brava coast on this fabulous wooden sailing boat equipped for up to ten passengers. The historically styled ship makes its way along the coast in an eight-hour journey to explore coves, caves and hidden beaches.
Sant Feliu de Guíxols. Tel: 97 232 3307. Approx. €45–110 per person.

Club Nàutic L'Escala
If you'd like to learn to sail, this is the place for you. The Club Nàutic offers sailing and yachting courses here in the Alt Empordà.
Port la Clota, L'Escala. Tel: 97 277 0016; www.nauticescala.com

Golfing in the Costa Brava

Getting away from it all

Kayaking Costa Brava

Guided kayaking excursions take you to hidden coves all along the Costa Brava. Trained instructors accompany the trips, which are geared towards beginners and last three to four hours. Courses are also available.

Carrer Enric Serra 42. Tel: 97 277 3806; www.kayakingcb.com. Excursions from approx. €40.

Viajes Orsom

Offering a variety of catamaran and boat hires, Viajes Orsom can organise full- or half-day outings around Barcelona.

Tel: 93 221 8283 or 93 441 0537; www.barcelona-orsom.com

Viento Sur

Hire yachts or sailing boats with or without a captain and set off to explore the vast Mediterranean. Based in Barcelona's port.

Tel: 600 456 680; email: viento.sur@ verizon.net. Approx. €400–600 per day.

Sightseeing from the air
JIP-Aviació

See the Costa Brava from the air with a short flight in a light aircraft. Flights last up to 30 minutes and cruise either over the northern end of La Costa Brava, where you'll be able to see Cadaqués and Cap de Creus, or over the southern end, where you'll spot the Illes Medes and L'Escala.

Aeródomo de Empuriabrava. Tel: 97 245 0111; www.jipaviacio.com.

The thrills of white-water rafting

Approx. €50–150 per passenger depending on length of flight & number of passengers.

Kon-Tiki

One of the best hot-air-balloon companies out there (and yes, there are a lot), Kon-Tiki offers flights of an hour or more covering practically any area of Catalonia. Transport and a full breakfast are included.

Tel: 639 206 454; www.globuskontiki.com. Flight average €150 per person.

Tours with a difference
Barcelona walking tours

Get the inside story on Barcelona's history with this fascinating walking tour of the Barri Gòtic. Tours are given daily in English; go to the tourist office in Plaça de Catalunya for more information.

Tel: 93 368 9700; www.barcelonaturisme.com. Tour approx. €8.

Bus Turístic Barcelona

Barcelona's two Bus Turístic routes make loops around the city, stopping

at most major attractions, providing an easy way to get around or just to get an overview of the sights. Your ticket is valid all day long, and you can get on and off as many times as you like. Get tickets at the tourist office or on the bus itself.
Tickets Adult/Child approx. €16/10.

Dofi Jet boat tours – Calella to Tossa

The *BlueEye*, a glass-bottomed boat, takes you from Calella to Tossa de Mar, allowing you to enjoy the scenery both above and below the water.
Carrer Sant Antoni 3. Tel: 97 235 2021; www.dofijetboats.com. Tours approx. €4–15.

El Molí bike tours – Penedès

Combining cycling and wine tourism, El Molí takes you through the low hills of the Penedès region, where vineyards fill the horizon and wineries provide welcome resting spots along the route. Just don't drink too much wine or you might topple right off your bike!
Alt Penedès. Tel: 93 897 2207; www.elmolitours.com. Excursion approx. €100–500.

Fat Tire Bike Tours Barcelona

See Barcelona on two wheels with the English-language tours led by Fat Tire. Offering day and night tours on easy-to-ride, comfortable bicycles, this is a fun alternative way to see the sights. You can rent bikes too. Credit cards are not accepted.
Tel: 93 301 3612.

www.fattirebiketoursbarcelona.com. Plaça George Orwell. Rental approx. €8/3 hours, tour approx. €25. Open: Tours given Sept–mid-Dec & mid-Mar–mid-Apr 12.30pm; mid-Apr–July 11.30am & 4.30pm; Aug 4pm.

Golondrines tour of Barcelona's ports

Tour Barcelona's ports on one of these comfortable pleasure cruises. The 35-minute ride takes you from the Port Vell to the Port Olímpic, and you'll enjoy a view of the city's shore and skyline along the way.
Portal de la Pau. Tel: 93 442 3106. Admission €4–10.

Torisme Vall d'Aran hiking tours

The tourist office of the Vall d'Aran offers eight different guided excursions along trails in the valley. Hike around lakes, visit abandoned mines or pass old sanctuaries and churches. These walks are all relatively easy and are appropriate for walkers of all ages and skill levels.
Vielha. Tel: 97 364 0110; www.aran.org. From approx. €30 per excursion.

Tren Turístic Roses-Cadaqués

This is a charming and fun way to enjoy the scenery between the two Costa Brava resort towns of Roses and Cadaqués. As you enjoy the sea and mountain scenery, a recorded narrative tells the region's history.
Carrer Pescadors 9, Roses. Tel: 97 215 2002; www.trenrosesexpres.com. Approx. €5 per hour.

Shopping

In recent years, shopping has become one of the most popular activities for visitors to Catalonia. Barcelona is simply loaded with unique, fashionable shops, making it one of the great shopping destinations of Europe. Beyond the city you'll find traditional shops, where local specialities are made.

Head to Barcelona for designer fashion, household goods or furniture, or simply to window-shop. Of course here you'll also be able to find shops selling many of the specialities from other parts of Catalonia. Popular buys in the region include ceramics (the Costa Brava town La Bisbal is famous for them), textiles, shoes, olive oil, sausage and wine. Locally designed clothing (*see pp148–9*) and jewellery are other good things to look out for.

Nearly everything mentioned below can be found in Spain's mega department store El Corte Inglés (The English Cut), *www.elcorteingles.es*. There are numerous branches in Catalonia, the most accessible being right on Plaça de Catalunya in Barcelona. They have everything from food to furniture, stocking goods as diverse as kitchenware, clothing, shoes, toys, baby goods, office supplies, books, electronics, CDs, appliances and souvenirs… the list goes on and on.

Paying

Spaniards (including Catalans) are famous for their aversion to credit cards. People here like to see the cash up front. That's probably why Spain has one of the world's highest concentrations of ATM machines – so that shoppers caught unawares can withdraw cash instead of using their card in a shop.

While most medium to large shops do accept popular credit cards such as Visa and MasterCard, you'll find plenty of small, family-run shops that want cash only. Produce markets, flea markets and street kiosks are other cash-only zones. Surprisingly, you may also be requested to pay in cash if you buy something unusually expensive, like furniture or art. The vendor simply doesn't want to risk not getting paid. In these cases, they might offer the article to you *sense rebut* (without a receipt), which means that they won't charge you tax, making it an unofficial sale.

Tax and tax refund

VAT (IVA, sales tax) in Spain is
16 per cent on most goods, though
it's only 7 per cent on food and
accommodation. Travellers from
outside the EU are lucky, because they
can reclaim the IVA. Simply request a
refund form showing what you bought,
how much IVA you paid, and where
you made the transaction. Present this
document, along with your passport
and boarding pass, to the customs
booth in the airport. They'll take your
documents and return your money in a
matter of weeks (or months).

Books

Books sold in Catalonia tend to be a
little more expensive than those sold in
other parts of Europe, but nevertheless
there is a decent bookstore culture.
You'll find books in English in El Corte
Inglés and in big chain bookshops like
FNAC (which also sells electronics) and
Casa del Llibre (there's a large branch
on Passeig de Gràcia in Barcelona).
Specialist bookshops selling used books
or books on topics ranging from travel
to design to women's issues are
scattered throughout Barcelona and
other large towns.

Ceramics

Most ceramics sold in Catalonia come
from La Bisbal, an inland Costa Brava
town that owes a huge chunk of its
economy to the pottery trade. Its main
street is lined with shops selling

Ceramics and other souvenirs on sale in La Bisbal

High-quality clothes are a Barcelona speciality

ceramics large and small. This is where the prices are best, but Bisbal ceramics are sold in other parts of Catalonia, too. In Barcelona, Art Escudellers (*Calle Escudellers 23. Tel: 93 412 6801*) is a virtual warehouse of ceramics and pottery from La Bisbal and elsewhere in Spain.

Clothing

Local designers abound (see *pp148–9*), making the region, especially Barcelona, an exceptional place to find original threads. The Barcelona district of La Ribera is a hotspot for designers, and on streets like Carrer del Rec you'll pass shop after shop showcasing upbeat, offbeat fashion. Make for boutiques such as MTX Barcelona (*Carrer Rec 32. Tel: 93 319 1398*) for funky women's fashions. The Custo Barcelona shop (*Plaça de les Olles 7. Tel: 93 268 7893*), selling the brand's tell-tale tee-shirts and wildly printed clothing, is another good stop.

The Barri Gòtic has also proved itself as a magnet for the fashionable, especially along streets like Carrer Fuencarrales, known for trendy shops geared towards a younger crowd, and Carrer Avinyò, packed with more sophisticated designs. Here visit Sugarhill (*Carrer Avinyò 6*), for reasonably priced but beautiful clothes and handmade leather bags.

International labels love Catalonia, too. In Barcelona stroll streets like Passeig de Gràcia (dubbed the 'Catalan Fifth Avenue') or Avinguda Diagonal for the top names in European fashion, including Emporio Armani, Chanel, Max Mara and Gucci.

Food and drink

There is no shortage of excellent food and drink available here. Catalan sausages are one of the more famous goodies; hotspots for dried sausages like *fuet* and *butifarra* are Vic and Cardona.

For olive oil, head down to El Priorat, where the olive oil DO Siurana makes some of the tastiest you'll ever try. Their tiny *arbequina* olives are responsible for this nectar, which can cost €5 and upwards a litre.

El Priorat is also famous for its wine (*see pp90–91*) and small shops and cooperatives throughout the region sell wine by the bottle or by the gallon, pumping it out of wooden barrels into plastic jugs for you to take home. Penedès is another good place to buy wine. Vilafranca del Penedès is home to countless top wine shops. For information on buying wine in Barcelona, *see p46*.

Shoes

Leather is quite good and cheap in Spain, so shoes are a big industry here. Many of the top shoe companies come from the historically Catalan island of Mallorca and have a strong presence in Catalonia. One of the best-known shoe brands is Camper (*www.camper.es*), known for their his-and-her, offbeat to cool, footwear that's actually comfortable to walk in. There are numerous Camper stores in Catalonia, most of them in Barcelona, such as the branch on La Rambla de Catalunya 122 (*tel: 93 217 2384*). For a more refined style, look out for Farrutx (*Rasellón 218. Tel: 93 215 0685 and Pau Casals 18–20. Tel: 93 200 6920; www.farrutx.es*).

Fresh fruit and veg at Barcelona's market on La Rambla

Catalan designers

Barcelona has long been recognised as a centre for art and design, so it only makes sense that fashion designers would begin popping up here too. The Mediterranean city isn't exactly synonymous with haute couture – yet – but young fashion designers are well on their way to ensuring Barcelona an enduring place on the world's fashion map.

You may not recognise these designer names, but chances are good that you've seen designs that imitate their style. Custo Barcelona, Josep Font, Lydia Delgado and Armand Basi are among the most talented and most popular Catalan designers. Their fanciful yet clean-lined styles are winning supporters and copy-cats all over the world, in the process earning Catalonia a name for fashion.

These designers are the modern face of Barcelona's long and lucrative textile industry. The city has hosted fashion shows since 1961 and has been an important textile centre for more than 200 years, yet only recently have designers cared much about attracting international attention.

The Mediterranean climate and culture, as well as the region's proximity to the rest of Europe, bring a light, international air to Catalonia that makes it a natural environment for creative development, supporters of Catalan design say. This vague and oft-used claim bears more weight when one considers the masters of art and design that have come from or worked in the area – Pablo Picasso, Salvador Dalí, Joan Miró and Antoni Gaudí, to name a few.

Who's who?
Custo Barcelona: Seen those cotton tee-shirts with a woman's face on the front, green and orange swirls on the back and crocheted sleeves? That's Custo. The label is known for casual, chic tee-shirts, but it has also moved into skirts and trousers and has

Barcelona fashions range from funky to *haute couture*

Antonio Miró fashion comes from the catwalk to the high street

expanded its designs for men. Find it at the signature store in the Barcelona neighbourhood called The Born (*93 268 7893*) or check out its website at *www.custobarcelona.com*

Armand Basi: Urban designs are the basis of the Armand Basi collection. Find them at the brand's shop in

Costume and everyday jewellery is a good buy in design-conscious Catalonia

Barcelona (*93 215 1421*) or online at *www.armandbasi.com*

Lydia Delgado: Known for her strong lines and bold use of colour, Lydia Delgado creates women's fashions that take guts to wear. Find her designs in designer boutiques.

Josep Font: Young, fun and one of the coolest designers working in Spain, Font's designs are inspired by history and a traditional Spanish look. Find them at his shop in Barcelona (*93 415 6550*) or online at *www.josepfont.com*

Antonio Miró: His style is modern and simple, with a focus on quality trousers, soft cottons and classic accessories. Find it at the Antonio Miró shops in Barcelona (*93 488 2800*) or online at *www.antoniomiro.es*

Entertainment

The options for entertainment in Catalonia are endless. In cities and larger towns you'll find a broad range of nightlife options, from quiet wine bars where you can sip a vino tinto *while chatting, to all-night* discotecas *that bump and grind till dawn. In small and large towns local festivals provide ideal entertainment. The spectacles are unique, fun and usually free.*

Cinema

Catalans love going to the movies, and you'll find cinemas in even the smallest towns. That said, nearly all of them show films in Spanish only. For English cinema you'll have to keep your eyes and ears open to talk of special showings. In Barcelona there are several original-version (VO) cinemas, including:

Casablanca Alternative film from throughout Europe, subtitled in Spanish. *(Passeig de Gràcia 115. Tel: 93 218 4345.)*

Verdi Cinema With a penchant for the quirky, this lively cinema shows a little bit of everything, from offbeat movies, to arty European films, to occasional Hollywood blockbusters. *(Carrer Verdi 32. Tel: 93 238 7990; www.cinemes-verdi.com)*

Yelmo Icària Cinema The place to find American, Hollywood-style movies, all with Spanish subtitles. *(Carrer de Salvador Espiriu 61. Tel: 93 221 7585.)*

Cultural events

Every town has its *feste major* (main festival), a few days or a week dedicated to partying. These festivals include parades, processions, lots of eating and the decidedly Catalan traditions of *castellers* (*see pp76–7*) and the *correfoc* (*see p22*). Some of the best festivals are held in Lleida in mid-May, Vilafranca del Penedès in August and Barcelona in late September. These are almost always accompanied by free outdoor concerts, fireworks displays and special cultural events. For more on festivals, *see pp22–3*.

Other interesting events include:

Barcelona

Barcelona's annual summer arts festival, El Grec, is an orgy of theatre, dance, music and art that begins in mid-June and lasts through July. Venues all over the city are included under this massive festival's umbrella, and the line-up usually includes top performers from Spain, other parts of Europe and overseas. *www.bcn.es*

Perallada

The Festival Internacional de Música held in Perellada's castle every July and August is a fantastic way to see this historic castle brought back to life. The festival focuses on lyrical singing, but the programme of 25 events runs the gamut from recitals and ballets to chamber music and opera. Find out more at *www.festivalperalada.com*

Sabadell

The Festival d'Òpera a Catalunya (Catalonia Opera Festival) is held in this town near Barcelona every season, staging different operas from October to May. Get more information from *tel: 93 725 6734; www.amics-opera-sabadell.es*

Sitges

The Sitges International Film Festival has been going on for 40 years, and it's beginning to draw serious attention from the international film world. With a focus on scary movies and thrillers, the festival draws together films from all over the world. The festival is held annually in autumn. *www.sitges.org*

Tarragona

The Concurs Internacional de Focs d'Artifici (International Fireworks Competition), when experts and fans from across the globe meet to shoot off elaborate fireworks, is held in July. For more information contact Tarragona's tourist office (*see p79*).

The Catalans love fiery festivals, often accompanied by big street parties

Flamenco

Catalonia is not the best place to see flamenco. Nearly all the shows here feature dancers and musicians imported from other places (mostly southern Spain), and the shows are attended almost exclusively by tourists. That said, the quality is not all that bad, and if you are willing to recognise that what you're seeing is not as authentic as it could be, watching a flamenco show can be an entertaining way to pass the evenings. In Barcelona head to spots like Tarantos, where some of Spain's top flamenco dancers have performed (after the flamenco show, stay on to dance to salsa and pop music until the wee hours), or Tablao Cordobés, offering a dinner show and very professional dancing and music.

Tarantos. Plaça Reial 17. Tel: 93 319 1789. Tablao Cordobés. La Rambla 35. Tel: 93 317 5711.

Bars, clubs and live music

Bars and clubs are found even in the smallest Catalan towns, where on weekends they fill with a largely young crowd out for a good time. For live music you'll probably have to make your way to Barcelona, where a variety of venues offer everything from classical music to jazz and rock and roll.

Barcelona

Gran Teatre del Liceu Barcelona's historic opera house, this is a city institution.
Las Ramblas 51–59. Tel: 93 485 9913.

Harlem Jazz Club This intimate concert venue is a fantastic place to catch jazz, fusion flamenco or blues shows.
Carrer de la Comtessa de Sobradiel 8. Tel: 93 310 0755.

L'Auditori de Barcelona One of Barcelona's most modern stages, this is the home of Barcelona's Symphony Orchestra and it boasts ideal acoustics for the symphony's complex musical arrangements. The Auditori is also used for rock and mainstream concerts.
Carrer Lepant 150. Tel: 93 247 9300.

London Bar Popular with expats, this bar has been around for nearly a century and is still drawing in crowds.
Carrer Nou de la Rambla 34. Tel: 93 318 5261.

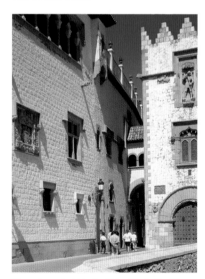

Concerts are held in the Palau Maricel in Sitges

Luz de Gas An old theatre turned club, you'll hear everything from jazz to country to rock and roll here. After about 1am, it's a standard disco catering to a slightly more mature crowd. *Carrer Muntaner 246. Tel: 93 414 1759.*

Girona
Girona's old quarter is packed with little bars and clubs that cater to the town's active student population. From Thursday to Saturday nights these places stay busy serving drinks and Spanish pop until late. Try Silent Block (*Carrer de Palafrugell 20*) if you want to dance in a laid-back setting.

Lleida
Carrer de Bonaire Lleida's low-key nightlife scene is centred around the central Carrer de Bonaire, where students and young professionals go to bar hop and find a spot to dance. Most places are open Thursdays to Saturdays with no fixed licensing hours.

Sitges
Palau Maricel Concerts and other special events are held regularly in this gorgeous Modernist building. The rooftop terrace offers views of the sea. *Carrer Fonollar. Tel: 93 894 0364.* No regular opening hours.

'Sin Street' Sitges is a hotspot for nightlife, and most of the town's bars and dance clubs are lined along one busy strip, the Carrer Dos de Maig, lovingly referred to as the *Calle del Pecado*, or 'Sin Street'. Float from bar to bar, enjoying a drink or dancing until 3am, when the street shuts down for the night. The crowd here is mixed; you'll find everyone from high school students to retired folk out for a night on the town.

Tarragona
Café Cantonada A laid-back bar with a pool table and a young crowd, this is a nice place for a drink or two. *Carrer de Fortuny 23. Tel: 97 721 3524.*

El Cau Near the Roman circus, this bar has more atmosphere, with music lasting late into the night on weekends. *Calle Trinquet Vall.*

Theatre
Most theatre is in Catalan, making it difficult for foreigners to really get a lot out of the performance. Nevertheless, all is not lost. Look out for unusual theatre and performance groups like La Fura dels Baus (*see next page*), Tricicle or Mal Pelo, all of whom perform without dialogue, so whether you speak Catalan or Cantonese you'll understand most of the show.

There are also a few small-scale English theatre groups scattered about. Barcelona is home to the largest English theatre, but towns like Sitges have their versions too. Though they may put on occasional performances, these groups tend to act more like clubs for theatre fans than genuine professional companies.

La Fura dels Baus

For the past 25 years Catalans have been enjoying the creative and often disturbing antics of La Fura dels Baus (The Fury of the Sewer Rats), an experimental performance group known for its in-your-face depictions of violence, sexuality and chaos on stage. It must be seen to be understood. La Fura dels Baus is proof of Catalans' open-mindedness and willingness to accept what others may shun. This experimental theatre group has been challenging audiences at home and abroad since the late 1970s with its aggressive performances and daring social messages. Barrages of sound, constant movement, weird stage props and moving images (recent performances included video clips and streaming text running throughout the show), the performances rely heavily on audience participation and aim to leave no one ambivalent about what they've seen.

This group of six middle-aged men got its start doing street performances, but La Fura was soon launched to the stage. In its early days, La Fura was known mainly for noise and on-stage nudity, which were intended to shake audiences out of their stupor and to reflect on the role of theatre in life (or so the group says).

In 1992 La Fura gave a wildly successful performance at the inauguration of the Olympic Games, and after that performances were adapted slightly to the new widespread appeal that La Fura dels Baus suddenly enjoyed. Shows became a bit more focused, and although it was (and is) still

Technology and digital effects are integral aspects of La Fura's experimental theatre

The 'floating cultural container' of *Naumaquia 1*

unashamedly weird, La Fura began to show slightly more method to its madness, creating shows that moved beyond visual and audio stimulation to include storylines and characters. One of their first such creations was *Faust 3.0*, later made into a film, which tells the classic story of the mad doctor. Yet don't think that La Fura has become conformist; another much-talked-about show, *XXX*, breaks all taboos about sex in a brazen show about sex in our age.

Yet the group also has a tame side. One of La Fura dels Baus' creations is *Naumaquia 1*, a family-friendly 'container of culture' that travels throughout the world sharing ideas through performance and exhibits centred on the theme of creation. The fact that performers are floating on a boat represents the fact that all floated in their mothers' wombs for nine months, the group says. The womb was the one place where people are truly happy, which parallels the freedom found in theatre.

Even when they're being conventional La Fura dels Baus manage to inject their projects with the quirkily insightful attitude that has made them one of Catalonia's best-loved performance groups. *Find out about the company at www.lafura.com*

Children

Keeping the children entertained is no problem here. In summer water parks and theme parks open up and down the Catalan coast, while in winter Barcelona's indoor aquarium or interactive science museum can provide fun for the young and old alike.

Aquabrava

Supposedly this is the largest wave pool in Europe. Measuring 100m by 80m (110 × 87yds), there's no doubting that it's a mammoth body of water. Water slides, fake beaches and play areas round out the offerings of this very children-friendly water park.
Carretera Cadaqués, Roses.
Tel: 97 225 4344; www.aquabrava.com.
Open: June–Sept 10am–7pm. Admission: approx. €9–15, according to height.

Aquadiver

This sprawling water park has a wave pool, a 'rough river', a huge man-made lake and a mammoth water slide dubbed the 'mountain roller coaster'. Older children will get a kick out of these big attractions, while the little ones can splash around in calmer pools.
Carretera Circumvallació, Platja d'Aro.
Tel: 97 281 8732; www.aquadiver.com.
Open: June–mid-Sept 10am–7pm.
Admission: approx. €13–23, according to height.

Aquapark Safari Aqualeón

So you can't decide whether to visit the waterslide or the zoo? Here you can do both. The park is a combination of a traditional water park and a zoo-like animal park, with safari routes that take you to see the animals living here. The parrot and reptile shows are especially popular.
Albinyana, Baix Penedès.
Tel: 97 768 7656; www.aqualeon.es.
Safari: Open daily 10am–6pm. Water park: Open daily 10.15am–6pm.
Admission charge.

L'Aquárium

Barcelona's aquarium is a fantastic place to learn more about the sea and marine life. The building itself is impressive, with touches like a glass tunnel that runs through the shark tank. Come here to gawp at the big fish and to learn more from the exhibits about the sea's history and future.
Moll d'Espanya, Barcelona. Tel: 93 221 7474; www.aquariumbcn.com.

Open: Oct–May Mon–Fri 9.30am–9pm,
Sat–Sun open until 9.30pm, June & Sept
9am–9.30pm, July & Aug 9am–11pm.
Admission charge. Metro: Drassanes.

Aquopolis

Offering all the usual suspects –
water slides, fake beaches, wave
pools and inner tubes – Aquopolis
is a small but fun water park with
attractions for younger and older
children. The highlight here is the
dolphin show, a coordinated routine
involving six dolphins.
Passeig Pau Casals 65, La Pineda.
Tel: 97 737 0258; www.aquopolis.es.
Open: early May–mid-Oct 11am–10pm
(closes earlier out of high season).
Admission charge.

Barcelona Zoo

See p48 for information on Barcelona's
small but interesting zoo.

Catalunya en Miniatura

So, you want to see all of Catalonia but
don't have the time to explore it from
end to end? No problem, just hop by
Catalunya en Miniatura to see small-
scale reproductions of the region's
most famous sights. There's a
1:25 scale model of La Sagrada
Familia, a reproduction of the
Monasteri de Montserrat, and waist-
high versions of various other churches
and monuments. This unique park
sounds rather kitsch, and it is. But it's
also a fun and informative virtual trip
around Catalonia.

Children

If all else fails, there's always the beach

Torrelles de Llobregat. Tel: 93 689 0960;
www.catalunyaenminiatura.com.
Open: 10am–6pm, closed Mon Nov–Feb.
Admission charge.

Centro Náutic Aiguadolç Vela

This sailing school in Sitges offers
special sailing courses for kids. Children
aged 7 to 14 are taken out on sailing
dinghies to learn the basics of sailing
(always with an instructor). As they
advance they can learn how to sail
catamarans and other craft too.
Port Esportiu d'Aiguadolç, Sitges.
Tel: 93 811 3105; www.advela.net.
Open: spring and summer. Courses
from approx. €120.

Illa Fantasia

A water park perfectly suited to the
8-and-unders, 'Fantasy Island' is a fun
place with five huge pools and a variety
of watery attractions including wave
pools, water slides, wading pools, foam,
sprinklers, rafts and more.
Vilassar de Dalt, Maresme, Barcelona.
Tel: 93 751 4553; www.illafantasia.com.
Open: mid-June–mid-Sept 10am–7pm.
Admission charge.

IMAX Port Vell

Barcelona's IMAX theatre offers a variety
of 3-D films shown on the colossal dome
here, called the Omnimax. The very size
of the screen combined with the effect of
the 3-D show makes this an impressive
spectacle for children and adults. Movies
include documentaries on the natural
world and on the human body.

Port Vell, Barcelona. Tel: 93 225 1111;
www.imaxintegral.com. Open: daily,
with morning, afternoon and evening
shows. Admission charge.

Marineland

Head to this fun water park for
entertainment and a learning
experience. There are waterslides here,
but once your thrill quotient is met you
can visit the marine zoo, where 300
animals representing 50 different
species live. The tropical birds are an
especially popular aspect of the zoo.
There are also shows featuring
dolphins, sea lions and walruses.
Carretera Malgrat a Palafolls, Palafolls.
Tel: 93 765 4802; www.marineland.es.
Open: Apr–Oct. Admission: adults
approx. €20, kids approx. €13.

Museu de la Ciència de Barcelona

A fabulous interactive museum on the
northern edge of Barcelona, the Science
Museum, run by the La Caixa
foundation, offers children fun ways to
learn about technology and the
scientific world. Almost everything here
is touchable, inviting children of all
ages to participate in the exhibits.
Passeig de Sant Joan, Barcelona. Tel: 93
212 6050; www.fundacio.lacaixa.es.
Open: Mon–Fri 9.30am–8pm, Sat
10.30am–7.30pm, Sun 10.30am–2.30pm.
Free admission.

Museu de la Xocolata

This museum covers the history of
chocolate from earliest times until the

present day, showing the changing ways in which it was made, examples of containers through the ages and creative designs made from chocolate. There is a room dedicated to chocolate making and an audiovisual presentation.
Calle Comerç 36. Tel: 93 268 7878; museu@patisseria.cat. Open: Mon & Wed–Sat 10am–7pm, Sun 10am–3pm. Admission charge.

El Parc de les Aus

More than 1,000 birds representing some 300 species live in this bird rescue and breeding centre. The lush park provides an attractive and authentic habitat for the birds, many of which are tropical. One of the most interesting things here is the toucan population; El Parc de les Aus is one of the few places where these birds have bred in captivity.
Vilassar de Mar. Tel: 93 756 6166; www.elparcdelesaus.com. Open: Tue–Sun 10am–8pm. Admission charge.

Tibidabo Funfair

For information on Barcelona's old-fashioned funfair, *see p59.*

Universal Mediterranean–Port Aventura and Costa Caribe

Divided into five zones, each representing a different part of the world, Port Aventura has all the rides, shops and attractions you could want.
See p85 for more on Catalonia's biggest theme park.

Waterworld

Yet another water park, this one boasts a 215m- (235 ft-) long rafting river and a huge 'water roller coaster' guaranteed to thrill. These attractions are most suitable for older children.
Carretera Vidreres, Lloret de Mar. Tel: 97 236 8613; www.waterworld.es. Open: May–Oct 10am–7pm. Admission: approx. €11–19, according to height.

Tibidabo's funfair also offers spectacular views over Barcelona

Sports

Catalonia is not an enclave of traditional Spanish sports like bullfighting, but you can watch one of Europe's top football teams, FC Barcelona, or get into the action yourself with cycling, swimming or other sports. See the Getting Away section (p138) for more ideas.

Participation sports

Cycling

Mountain and road biking are popular in Catalonia, and there are many places along the coast and in the interior where you'll find good trails. For information on trails and services offered to bikers, contact the Catalan Cycling Federation at *www.fedecat.com* or the Centres BTT (Mountain Biking Centres) at *www.gencat.net/turisme/btt*. Centres BTT are set up along trails throughout Catalonia, offering guiders and assistance to mountain bikers.

Golf

Most of Catalonia's golf courses are on the Costa Brava, an area known for its quality courses. Several international golf tournaments are held here each year. Some of the best courses include:

Club Golf de Pals This lush, tree-lined course is challenging thanks to its layout and abundance of water.
Carretera Palafrugell a Torroella, km 13.6. Tel: 97 276 1835; www.clubgolfdepals.com

Golf Empordá With a variety of styles in holes and greenways, this course hosts many competitions and events each year. *Carretera de Palafrugell a Torroella. Tel: 97 276 0450; www.empordagolfclub.es*

Golf Serres de Pals Two kilometres ($1^1/_4$ miles) off the Mediterranean, this well-kept course sits atop rolling hills and is known as a solid but not overly challenging course. *Pals. Tel: 97 263 7375; www.golfserresdepals.com*

Swimming

Catalan beaches are generally very clean and are fine places to swim in warm weather. Look out for the coloured signs that give information about the cleanliness of the water and sand that day. Blue is 'very good', green is 'good', yellow is 'moderate', orange is 'deficient' and red is 'poor'. Barcelona's beaches are dirtier than most, but throughout the Costa Brava and Costa Daurada you'll find good swimming beaches.

Water sports

Windsurfing and sailing, among other watery sports, are very popular along the Catalan coasts. In resorts like Palafrugell, Roses, Sitges and Salou you'll find companies hiring windsurfs and sailboats. Many of these companies also offer courses. See the Getting Away section for more information, *pp141–2.*

Spectator sports
Bullfighting

Bullfighting is on its way out in Catalonia. Children aged 14 and under are forbidden to see the bloody, although traditional, spectacle, and the town hall has declared Barcelona an 'anti-bullfighting city', though it has yet to officially ban the sport. Until it does, you can still see bullfights staged on Sunday evenings from April through September in the city bullring.
La Monumental. Tickets cost approx.

€18 and upwards. Plaza Monumental. Gran Via de les Corts Catalanes. Tel: 93 245 5802.

Football

Catalonia's premier football club is the Fútbol Club Barcelona, 'Barça' to its fans, which plays in Barcelona's Camp Nou stadium. You can get tickets for regular season games through the Servicaixa service by calling 902 189 900 or buying online at *www.servicaixa.com.* While it's not hard to get tickets to most matches, you've got to be either extremely lucky or very well connected to obtain tickets for the big games like Barça v. Real Madrid.

Other Catalan football teams include RCD Espanyol (Barcelona's second team), CE Sabadell and Terrassa FC. RCD Espanyol plays in the Olympic Stadium on Montjuïc.
Camp Nou. Carrer Arístides Maillol gates 7 & 9. Tel: 93 496 3608; www.fcbarcelona.com. Metro: Camp Nou. Estadi Olímpic. Passeig Olímpic 17–19. Tel: 902 666 902; www.rcdespanyol.com. Metro: Espanya.

Windsurfing in the Costa Brava area is a popular pastime for natives and tourists alike

Food and drink

With its fish-and-vegetable Mediterranean diet and abundance of game in the interior, traditional Catalan cuisine uses fresh ingredients and a few basic herbs like thyme and rosemary. But Catalonia is also famous for its innovative, modern cuisine. Thanks to a movement led by chef Ferran Adrià (see pp112–13), Catalan cuisine has become one of the world's most celebrated.

Traditionally Catalan cuisine is based on the staples of wheat, oil and wine, a fact that has changed little over the region's long history. Many local dishes also show influences from Arab cuisine; as in Arab cooking, adding nuts and dried fruits is a popular way to enhance flavour. Catalan style has also been heavily influenced by its neighbour France and, more recently, by international flavours from America and Asia.

Vegetarians are catered for in many restaurants in Barcelona, but non-meat options can be harder to find elsewhere in the rest of Catalonia.

Local cuisine varies widely, depending on the area: there are the seafood dishes of the shore, the gamey meats of the countryside, the surf-'n'-turf creations common across central Catalonia, and the more sophisticated and international cuisine of Barcelona and the cities. Some of the most common Catalan dishes and sauces are listed here.

Allioli A strong garlic mayonnaise.

Butifarra A tasty, traditional sausage usually eaten grilled with white beans.

Calçots Served only in winter, these long onions are burnt to a crisp over an open fire, then peeled by hand and eaten dipped into a tangy *romesco*.

Conill i Cargols Rabbit and snails stewed together.

Crema Catalana Creamy custard topped with burnt sugar. Similar to *crème brûlée*.

Escalivada Roasted peppers, onions, tomatoes and aubergine served cold atop *pa amb tomàquet*.

Escudella A hearty, traditional stew characterised by its use of *butifarra* sausages. Pasta may be added.

Fideuá Seafish stew with squid, prawns and clams with tiny noodles, cooked then grilled. Eaten with *allioli*.

Pa amb tomàquet Thick slices of country bread smeared with tomato, olive oil and salt.

Paella Saffron, olive oil and rice cooked with shellfish.

Romesco A sauce made with tomato, garlic, almonds and dried pepper.

Suquet A tomato-based seafood stew.

What and when to eat

Catalans usually have very little for breakfast, often eating nothing at home and then making a leisurely stop for coffee and a pastry around 10am at a neighbourhood bar. Lunch was traditionally eaten at home and was followed by a short siesta. The realities of working hours and commuting have all but obliterated that healthy tradition, and now many people eat their lunch out, taking advantage of the good-value *menús*, set-price, three-course lunches available at restaurants all over Catalonia. The lunch hour begins about 1.30pm and lasts until 3pm or 3.30pm. You may have a hard time finding something to eat before or after that time. Dinner, if eaten at home, is a light affair. Boiled vegetables, soup or bread topped with ham or cheese are common. Yet when Catalans dine out they do it in style, arriving at around 10pm and feasting on two or three courses.

Eating out

Catalans love to eat out, and you'll find top-quality restaurants hiding in even the most unsuspecting nooks and crannies. We've chosen some of the best or most enjoyable eateries, but it is no exaggeration to say that Catalonia is a gourmand's paradise.

Catalan cheese comes in many varieties at the various produce markets

Where to eat

The following symbols have been used as a guide to price ranges, excluding drinks:

★	under €25 per person
★★	from €25–45 per person
★★★	from €46–60 per person
★★★★	over €60 per person

Arties

Casa Irene ★★★

Hands down the best restaurant in the Vall d'Aran, this is supposedly one of the King of Spain's favourite restaurants. The rustic mountain atmosphere contrasts with elegant fare like foie gras with Cornish hen eggs.
Carrer Major 4.
Tel: 97 364 4364;
www.hotelcasairene.com

Barcelona

Àbac ★★★

For many diners, this is the best restaurant in Barcelona. The service is excellent, the ingredients unbeatable, and the unique dishes, such as foie gras steamed in bamboo, are divine.
Carrer Rec 79–89.
Tel: 93 319 6600.

Bar Bodega Fortuny ★

For healthy food like cous-cous and hummus, head to this quirky restaurant. The lunch *menú* is good value (but be warned that service is very slow!).
Carrer Fortuny 31.
Tel: 93 317 9892.

Cal Pep ★★

If you can only go to one tapas bar in Barcelona, let it be this classic place, known for its amazing seafood. Be prepared to wait; Cal Pep is always packed.
Plaça de les Olles 8.
Tel: 93 310 7961.

Café de l'Acadèmia ★★

A cosy little place in the heart of the Barri Gòtic, this is a great place to come for quality Catalan fare for lunch or dinner.
Carrer Lledó 1.
Tel: 93 319 8253.

Coses de Menjar ★★

The décor goes beyond creative: small tables hang as chandeliers and the menus are presented on wine bottles. The food is inventive and fresh.
Pla de Palau 7.
Tel: 93 310 6001.

Els Quatre Gats ★★

The tavern made famous by Modernist artists, Els Quatre Gats is now a classy restaurant serving elegant tapas and traditional Catalan dishes.
Carrer Montsió 3.
Tel: 93 302 4140.

Espai Sucre ★★

If you always wanted to eat your dessert first, now you can. 'Sugar Place' is a fabulous restaurant where dessert is dinner.
Carrer Princesa 53.
Tel: 93 268 1630.

Laie Librería Café ★

Above a bookstore that boasts a great English section, Laie has a fantastic indoor/outdoor seating area and offers a delicious lunch buffet packed with options for vegetarians.
Carrer Pau Claris 85.
Tel: 93 302 7310;
www.laie.es

L'Hostal de Rita ★

Designed for those who want a quick, tasty lunch but don't want to spend much money on it, this stylish restaurant just off Passeig de Gràcia is a

great option. There's always a queue to get in.
Carrer Aragó 279.
Tel: 93 487 2376.

Los Caracoles ★★
A Barcelona classic for generations, this character-filled restaurant specialises in *caracoles* (snails), though they also do a mean roasted chicken (which you can see and smell as it sizzles on a spit right on the street corner) and tasty seafood dishes.
Carrer Escudellers 14.
Tel: 93 302 3185.

Maria Cristina ★★★
An excellent seafood restaurant, this is a calm, quiet place with

impeccable service and a focus on quality seafood that always manages to surprise.
Carrer Provença 269.
Tel: 93 215 3237.

Restaurante Vegetariano Arco Iris ★★
One of the better vegetarian restaurants Barcelona has to offer.
Roger de Flor 216.
Tel: 93 458 2283.

Berga
Sala ★★
The area around Berga is known for its wide variety of mushrooms, and the kitchen at Sala knows how to prepare them to perfection.

Paseo de la Pau 27.
Tel: 93 821 1185.

Besalú
Pont Vell ★★
Modern Catalonian fare overlooking the river in a rustic medieval setting.
Carrer Pont Vell 24.
Tel: 97 259 1027.

Cadaqués
La Galiota ★★
La Galiota has a long tradition of serving Catalan market cuisine. Offering delicious local seafood as well as inland specialities like pâté, this is a sure bet.
Carrer Narcís Monturiol 9. Tel: 97 225 8187.

Caldes de Montbui
Robert de Nola ★
This cosy restaurant is shaking things up in the traditional town of Caldes de Montboi. Using local ingredients, the chef creates a number of unexpected flavour combinations, such as country-style *canelones* (Catalan cannelloni) filled with prawns.
Passeig del Remei 48–50.
Tel: 93 865 4047.

Berga is famous for the quality and variety of its mushrooms

Figueres

Durán ★

Eat among old wine barrels and Castilian-style décor in this homely restaurant. Hearty dishes like cabbage stuffed with *butifarra* sausage are the basis of the varied menu here.
Carrer Lasauca 5.
Tel: 97 250 1250.

Empordà ★★★

Considered the top restaurant in town, this is a local institution known for its balance of tradition and innovation. The original chef here, Josep Mercader, was a pioneer in bringing French-style nouvelle cuisine to Catalonia.
Antigua Carretera de Francia. Tel: 97 250 0562;
www.hotelemporda.com

Girona

Albereda ★★

A comfortable place with a rustic style and low brick arches running through the dining room, Albereda offers an elegant Catalan fare, with an obvious French influence. Closed Sundays.
Carrer Albereda 9.
Tel: 97 222 6002.

Pil.la ★★

Small vegetarian restaurant, one of the few to be found outside Barcelona. Worth a try.
Sant Narcis, 65.
Tel: 97 223 4545.

El Celler de Can Roca ★★★

Run by three Catalan brothers, chefs Joan, Joseph and Jordi, this is one of Catalonia's best restaurants, and it has two Michelin stars to prove it. Creative and expertly elaborated dishes using local seafood and produce

Wherever there is space you'll find an outdoor café

form the basis of a menu that's reliably delicious yet always surprising.
Carretera de Taialà 40. Tel: 97 222 2157.

La Seu d'Urgell
El Castell ★★★
Forming part of an elegant hotel, El Castell has a Michelin star in recognition of its top-quality, creative gourmet cuisine. The décor, like the food, is sophisticated and promises a meal to remember.
Carretera N260, km 229. Tel: 97 335 0000.

Lleida
La Pérgola ★★
One of the most renowned restaurants in Lleida, La Pérgola is an elegant option with a good wine list and elaborate dishes such as stewed monkfish with cod tripe.
Paseo de Ronda 123. Tel: 97 323 8237.

Montseny
Can Barrina ★★
This hotel and restaurant in the Parc de Montseny is an inviting mountain refuge. The chef sources

Head to the local market for Catalonia's excellent cooked and cured meat

all produce locally from fish to fowl to fungi. There is a wide variety of home-made desserts and a large wine cellar.
Carretera de Palautordera. Tel: 93 847 3065.

Olot
Les Cols ★★
This sleek, ultra-stylish restaurant is the last thing you'd expect to find just outside provincial Olot. If you come, dress the part and be prepared to enjoy mouth-watering

modern versions of classic Catalan fare.
Carretera de la Canya. Tel: 97 226 9209.

Palafrugell
La Xicra ★★★★
You'll feel like you've gone to *avia*'s (grandma's) house when you step into this homely, traditional-style eatery. Tasty local specialities fill the menu, many of them featuring *mar i muntanya* (surf 'n' turf) combinations so popular here.
Carrer Estret 17. Tel: 97 230 5630.

Racó de Can Fabes is one of the greatest restaurants in Catalonia

Pals
Sa Punta ★★
Attached to the hotel of the same name, this classy restaurant uses fresh local seafood in most of its dishes, like the seafood lasagna and fish tartare.
Urbanizació Sa Punta. Tel: 97 263 6410; www.hotelsapunta.com

Roses
El Bulli ★★★★
A legend. For details *see p113*.

Salou
Albatros ★★
Fresh seafood is served year-round at this homely restaurant, and in season you can also get great game dishes. The terrace is a lovely place to sit in summer.
Carrer Brusselles 60. Tel: 97 738 5070.

Sant Celoni
Racó de Can Fabes ★★★★
One of the best restaurants in Catalonia, the Racó de Can Fabes, run by chef Santi Santamaría, has earned three Michelin stars, and it's not hard to see why. Impeccable service and presentation accompany exquisite dishes that change constantly. To try everything, ask for the *menú de degustació*.
Carrer Sant Joan 6. Tel: 93 867 2851.

Sitges
La Masía ★
Housed in an old farmhouse, this rustic

restaurant is an ideal place to try seasonal Catalan dishes. One of the best features is the innovative 'sausage tree' they bring at the beginning of the meal.
Passeig de Vilanova 164. Tel: 93 894 1076.

El Fresco ★★
The décor of El Fresco – artistic and perfectly Mediterranean – is the first thing that catches your attention here. When it arrives the food, a combination of local and international flavours, will win you over as well.
Carrer Pau Barrabeig 4. Tel: 93 894 0600.

Tarragona
Les Coques ★★
Near the cathedral, Les Coques is a classic restaurant serving mostly seafood from the coasts nearby. Try the *pulpitos* (tiny octopus), which are delicious.
Bajada del Patriarca 2. Tel: 97 722 8300.

Merlot ★★
This stylish restaurant in the city's old quarter offers a whopping choice of 2,000 wines. The food

is impressive too, with unexpected creations like tomato soup with garlic and tulips.
Carrer Cavallers 6. Tel: 97 722 0652.

Tossa de Mar
La Cuina de Can Simon ★★
Of the dozens of restaurants that fill the town, this is one of the best choices. Choose from local fish, traditional Catalan food and international dishes like their delicious risotto. Run by the Lores family.
Carrer Portal 24. Tel: 97 234 1269.

Vic
Jordi Parramon ★★★
The décor defines rustic elegance and the food fits perfectly with the theme. Ingredients from the Catalan countryside are presented honestly but creatively, making for a memorable dining experience in Vic.
Carrer Cardona 7. Tel: 93 886 3815.

Vilafranca del Penedès
Cal Ton ★★
This stylish place has a

great atmosphere, with an indoor–outdoor feel that tricks you into thinking you're eating on a terrace. Tasty local specialities like cod salad with *xató* sauce and duck with wine sauce are temptingly presented.
Carrer Casal 8. Tel: 93 890 3741.

Casa Joan ★★★
One of the most popular restaurants in town, Casa Joan offers a similar style to Cal Ton, with dishes that are creative versions of the traditional standards. The atmosphere is warm and friendly, with a lot of regulars.
Plaza de l'Estació 8. Tel: 93 890 3171.

Vilanova i la Geltrú
La Fitorra ★
A fabulous seafood restaurant, La Fitorra's elegance makes you feel as though you're eating in someone's private dining room. This is a great place to order paella.
Carrer Isaac Peral 8. Tel: 93 815 1125.

Local markets

Local produce markets are an essential part of Catalan culture, and nearly every town big or small has its covered market where you can buy locally grown fruit, fresh fish from the Mediterranean, cheeses, meat, olives and more.

Market shopping is an activity in itself, and if you go slowly and buy a lot, it can easily fill up an entire morning. Go to the individual fruit, cheese, meat and fish stalls, making polite small talk before telling the stallholder what you're looking for. In most places the vendors are extremely helpful people, offering ideas on how to prepare the food you buy and telling you what's in season and what is not quite ready to eat.

A large variety of cheeses on sale

Some of the most typical things to buy at Catalan markets are Spanish cheeses, like strong *manchego* or mild *mató*, a fresh cheese often served with honey. Locally grown tomatoes are another good buy, as are apricots, peaches, strawberries and cherries (in season), all grown in Catalonia, mostly around Lleida. Tiny *arbequina* olives come from the Priorat region and are some of the tastiest available. In autumn, you have to try the mushrooms that pop up in Catalan forests. One of the most typical of the region is the large, flavourful *rovellón*. In winter, you can buy the long

A selection of local honeys

A market stall in Mercat de la Boqueria, Barcelona

onions used for calçots. Common fish include *merluza* (hake) and *dorada* (bream). For shellfish try mussels or shrimp, both farmed in local waters.

Catalan sausages like *butifarra* and *butifarra negra* (blood sausage) are delicious. Spanish *jamon serrano* (salt-cured ham) is another must-try.

Market vocabulary

The following common phrases are listed first in Catalan and then in Spanish.

I would like	Voldria	Me gustaria
Do you have...?	Tenen?	¿Tienen?
Where can I buy...?	On puc ¿comprar...?	¿Dónde puedo ¿comprar?
How much is this?	Quant val això?	¿Cuánto vale?
Is it ripe?	Es madur?	¿Está maduro?

Hotels and accommodation

Catalonia offers a wide selection of accommodation options, from the stylish boutique hotels of Barcelona to the rustic inns of the countryside and the resort-style hotels of the coast. Spain's own star rating system is helpful too. Though prices vary widely between hotels, even if they have the same number of stars, you can expect one- and two-star hotels to have little or no amenities, while three- and four-stars will have extras like air conditioning, a restaurant and perhaps a pool. Across Spain, some of the nicest hotels available are the government-run Paradores, which are often housed in historic palaces or monasteries. Staying in a Parador is always a treat, as the service, food and style are always above par. Get more information at www.parador.es

Reservations

Booking is usually available online at the larger hotels, but smaller hotels will ask that you reserve by phone or fax. You'll find that they'll usually require a credit card number to make a reservation.

Prices

The guide prices here are based on a typical double room, including tax but not normally breakfast.

★   under €100
★★   €101–180
★★★   over €180

Artíes

Parador de Turisme ★★

A short drive from the slopes of the Baqueira-Beret ski resort, this elegant hotel is ideal for relaxing after a hard day spent skiing or hiking. *Carretera Baqueira-Beret. Tel: 97 364 0801; www.parador.es*

Barcelona

Banys Orientals ★

With its sleek décor and ideal location near the cathedral and the Ribera district, this is a great hotel at a great price. *Carrer de la Argenteria 37. Tel: 93 268 8460; www.hotelbanysorientals. com*

Colon ★★

Overlooking Barcelona's cathedral, this classy hotel is one of the most romantic spots in the city. Old-world elegance oozes out of every corner. *Avinguda de la Catedral 7. Tel: 93 301 1404; www.hotelcolon.es*

Gran Hotel La Florida ★★★

Without a doubt one of the top hotels in Barcelona, La Florida is perched on Tibidabo mountain and offers splendid views of the city below.

Carretera Vallvidrera 83–93. Tel: 93 259 3000; www.hotellaflorida.com

Inglaterra ★

Sitting right between Las Ramblas and L'Eixample, the Inglaterra is in a perfect location. Rooms are stylish and airy, and the service is good (especially considering the low price).

Carrer Pelai 14.
Tel: 93 35 0511;
www.hotel-inglaterra.com

Cadaqués
Playa Sol ★★

Rooms are simple and the extras are few and far between, but this homely hotel offers amazing views of the bay and is a very relaxing place.

Platja Pianc 5.
Tel: 97 125 8100;
www.playasol.com

Calella de Palafrugell
Garbí ★

Overlooking the wide beach of Calella, this large hotel offers all the basic services you would need for a fantastic seaside holiday.

Passeig de les Roques 3.
Tel: 97 261 4040;
www.hotelgarbi.com

Castelldefels
Hesperia Castelldefels ★★

Right on the Castelldefels beach, this family hotel is a comfortable option that puts you close to Barcelona and to the sea.

The luxurious Gran Hotel La Florida in Barcelona

Hotels and accommodation

Passeig Maritim 138.
Tel: 93 636 2450;
www.hoteles-hesperia.es

Figueres
Empordà ★★
Home to the city's top restaurant, this cosy hotel sits just 1km ($^1/_3$ mile) outside the centre and is a great place to stay if you're looking for peace and quiet. The interior is comfortable but elegant.
Carretera N-11 km 763.
Tel: 97 250 0562;
www.hotelemporda.com

Girona
Carlemany ★
This big, sleek hotel is low on charm but high on practicality. With good service, a central location and all the extras, it's a convenient choice.
Plaça de Miquel Santaló.
Tel: 97 221 1212;
www.carlemany.es
Hotel Costabella ★★
A quaint yellow farmhouse outside the city, this is the perfect weekend retreat. Comfortable, if standard, rooms and a good restaurant make the Costabella a solid bet.
Avinguda Fraça 61.

Tel: 97 220 2524;
www.hotelcostabella.com

La Seu d'Urgell
Parador de Turisme ★★
This gorgeous hotel next to the town's cathedral is the best place to stay in this part of Catalonia. Keep an eye open for the pretty Renaissance plaza in its centre, and have a meal in the elegant restaurant here; one of the specialities is snails.
Carrer Sant Domenec 6.
Tel: 97 335 2000;
www.parador.es

L'Estartit
Bell Aire ★
This simple hotel offers sunny rooms (try to get one on an upper floor for a view of the Mediterranean) and friendly service. The beach is a short walk away.
Carrer Església 39.
Tel: 97 275 1302;
www.hotelbellaire.com

Lleida
AC Lleida ★★
The sleek AC Lleida is near all the attractions of the city and offers the top style and service that the

AC chain is known for.
Carrer Unió 8. Tel: 97 328 3910; www.ac-hoteles.com

Salou
H10 Salauris Palace ★★★
The sprawling Salauris Palace has stylish, modern rooms and a fantastic pool and terrace area. The beach is about a ten-minute walk away.
Avinguda Països Catalanes. Tel: 97 738 8908; www.h10.es

Sitges
Romántic ★
This little hotel truly is romantic. With its Modernist façade and homely feel, you'll never want to leave. The hotel is located in the heart of town, a ten-minute walk from the beach.
Carrer Sant Isidre 33.
Tel: 93 894 8375;
www.hotelromantic.com
Melià Gran Sitges ★★★
One of the town's top hotels, the large, pyramid-shaped Gran Sitges is popular with business travellers in winter and with those on holiday in summer. Rooms are elegant and functional, and there's a

large pool to use on days when you don't want to take the short walk to the beach.
Port d'Aiguadolç 8. Tel: 93 811 0811; www.solmelia.com

Tarragona
AC Tarragona HH
This is a great hotel if you want to be close to Tarragona's historic sights. The rooms are fresh and modern.
Avinguda de Roma 8. Tel: 97 747 7105; www.ac-hoteles.com
Lauria ★
If you want to be right in the middle of things, this modest hotel is a perfect choice. Rooms are comfortable though not grand, but the best thing about the Lauria is its location right on the city's Rambla. The beach is a couple of kilometres out of town, but there is a small pool at the hotel.
Rambla Nova 20. Tel: 97 723 6712; www.hlauria.es

Vic
Parador de Turisme ★★
Sitting outside the town centre, this lovely hotel overlooks a lake and is a great base if you want to tour Catalonia's interior.
Paraje el Bac de Sau. Tel: 93 812 2323; www.parador.es

Vielha
Melià Royal Tanau ★★★
A luxurious five-star with all the trimmings, this mountain inn has a cosy feel, with a spacious sitting area, complete with fireplace, downstairs. Rooms are done in an all-wood mountain theme, and many have large bathtubs perfect for soaking in after the day's exertions. A bonus of this hotel is the ski lift that's literally right outside the door.
Carretera de Beret, Vall d'Aran. Tel: 97 364 446; www.solmelia.com

Hotels and accommodation

The Melià Royal Tanau in Vielha is a great place to spend a Pyrenean winter holiday

Practical guide

Arriving

Getting into Spain is very easy for
residents of the EU. You need only
your passport to stay for up to three
months or less. The same goes for US,
Canadian, Australian and New Zealand
citizens. If you want to stay longer
you'll have to begin the tedious process
of declaring residency here, something
relatively simple for EU citizens, but a
very complicated process for those
living outside the EU.

By air

Catalonia's main airport is Barcelona's
Aeroport del Prat, which is a 20-minute
drive from the Catalan capital. This
busy airport has three terminals and a
steady stream of flights coming in from
across the globe. It takes about two
hours to fly here from the UK. easyJet
flies here from London, Liverpool,
Bristol and Newcastle. Monarch and

Jet2 also operate flights. Secondary
airports are in Girona, which is about
one hour north of Barcelona and gives
easy access to the Costa Brava, and
Reus, an hour south of the city, near
Tarragona. The rise of budget airlines
has given these small, provincial
airports a new lease of life. Ryanair flies
to both Girona and Reus from several
UK and Irish airports.

By rail

Catalonia is well connected to the rest
of Spain and Europe by rail. You can
get here from Paris in about 9 hours,
and from here head to Madrid in about
5 hours. There are major stations in
Girona, Barcelona, Lleida and
Tarragona. From those four cities you
can branch out and take regional or
cercanías (local) trains to the
surrounding towns. The only area of
Catalonia without adequate rail

Catalonia enjoys an efficient local and long-distance rail network

coverage is the Pyrenees, where the steepness of the slopes have impeded the railway's advancement.

By road

The A-7 motorway comes into Catalonia from France and runs through Girona, Barcelona and Tarragona before heading on to the Ebro Delta and Valencia. This is the easiest and most common way to enter Catalonia by car, though be sure you budget for the many tolls on this road; they really add up!

By sea

Barcelona is the Mediterranean's busiest port, and large ships (mostly cruise ships) come in daily. There are also a few ferries operating, like those of Trasmediterránea (*www.trasmediterranea.es*), which connect the city with the Balearic Islands. There are a few other Mediterranean ferries with stops here too.

Camping

Camping is widely available in Catalonia. Most campsites will charge you according to the number of people in your group and the number of tents and cars with you. Prices begin at about €4 per person, but can be more than double that in the more popular campsites, especially during the busy month of August.

Some of the most popular places to camp are along the coast and in the

Pyrenees. The Catalan tourist office publishes an annual guide to all campsites in the region. You can buy or refer to it at several tourist offices across Catalonia.

Climate

Most of Catalonia enjoys a mild Mediterranean climate, with long, warm summers and cool winters throughout most of the region. The Pyrenees, however, have a very different climate, since many of the weather systems that arrive here come over from the Atlantic coast rather than from the Mediterranean.

Consulates

In Barcelona you'll find the British Consulate (*Avinguda Diagonal 477. Tel: 93 366 6200;*

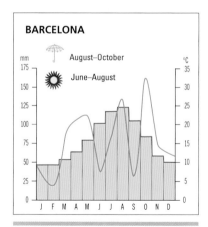

BARCELONA

August–October

June–August

WEATHER CONVERSION CHART

25.4mm = 1 inch

$°F = 1.8 × °C + 32$

www.ukinspain.com/english.
Open: Mon–Fri 8.30am–3pm in
summer) and the US Consulate
(*Passeig Reina Elisenda de Montcada 23.*
Tel: 93 280 2227;
http://barcelona.usconsulate.gov.
Open: Mon–Fri 9am–1pm). For other
countries you will need to contact the
Madrid embassies:
Australia Plaza del Descubridor Diego
de Ordás 3, Metro Ríos Rosas.
Tel: 91 353 6600; www.embaustralia.es
Canada Calle Núñez de Balboa 35,
Metro Velázquez.
Tel: 91 423 3250; www.canada-es.org
Republic of Ireland Paseo de la
Castellana 46, Metro Rubén Dario.
Tel: 91 436 4093; email:
embajadairlanda@terra.es
New Zealand Plaza de la Lealtad 2,
Metro Banco de España.
Tel: 91 523 0226; email:
nzembmadrid@santandersupernet.com

Crime

Crime is not a huge problem in
Catalonia, but you do need to be on
guard against pickpockets and petty
thieves. Tourist areas, public transport,
Internet cafés, ATMs and hotel lobbies
are the places where thieves are most
likely to be prowling. Be sure to watch
your belongings at all times; don't
leave bags out of sight on the beach
or at restaurants. In the street, be sure
to keep your wallet in a front pocket
and always carry a handbag that zips.
Lock all car and hotel room doors,
and keep valuables out of sight.
See also First Steps, *p28*, for advice on
common scams.

It's a good idea to carry just one
credit card and only a copy of your
passport, leaving extra cards and the
passport itself locked in your hotel safe
or kept in another secure place.
Likewise, don't carry lots of cash; if you

The Generalitat in Barcelona, Catalonia's seat of government

must carry it, avoid keeping it all in your wallet – here it will probably be visible each time you open your wallet to pay for something.

If you are a victim of crime, you should contact the National Police immediately to report it. (*See p183 for police and other emergency numbers.*)

Currency

Catalonia, like the rest of Spain, uses the euro (€). Since the euro was introduced in 2002 prices on everything from food to museums have gone up considerably, in some cases as much as 30 per cent. Still, Spain tends to be more affordable than northern European countries.

Currency exchange and ATMs

Banks offer the best exchange rates and are easily spotted throughout Catalonia. If you arrive after 2pm, when banks close, you can withdraw money from the ATM, though your own bank may apply its own exchange rate and possibly a surcharge. Avoid *casas de cambio* (exchange bureaux), which usually charge exorbitant rates and are often surrounded by opportunistic pickpockets waiting for tourists to emerge with a wad of euros.

Customs regulations

Customs regulations differ depending on where you're arriving from. If you're coming to Spain from another EU country you can bring in 800 cigarettes, 200 cigars or 1kg (2.2lb) of tobacco,

CONVERSION TABLE

FROM	TO	MULTIPLY BY
Inches	Centimetres	2.54
Feet	Metres	0.3048
Yards	Metres	0.9144
Miles	Kilometres	1.6090
Acres	Hectares	0.4047
Gallons	Litres	4.5460
Ounces	Grams	28.35
Pounds	Grams	453.6
Pounds	Kilograms	0.4536
Tons	Tonnes	1.0160

To convert back, for example from centimetres to inches, divide by the number in the third column.

MEN'S SUITS

UK	36	38	40	42	44	46	48
Catalonia & Rest of Europe	46	48	50	52	54	56	58
USA	36	38	40	42	44	46	48

DRESS SIZES

UK	8	10	12	14	16	18
France	36	38	40	42	44	46
Italy	38	40	42	44	46	48
Catalonia & Rest of Europe	34	36	38	40	42	44
USA	6	8	10	12	14	16

MEN'S SHIRTS

UK	14	14.5	15	15.5	16	16.5	17
Catalonia & Rest of Europe	36	37	38	39/40	41	42	43
USA	14	14.5	15	15.5	16	16.5	17

MEN'S SHOES

UK	7	7.5	8.5	9.5	10.5	11
Catalonia & Rest of Europe	41	42	43	44	45	46
USA	8	8.5	9.5	10.5	11.5	12

WOMEN'S SHOES

UK	4.5	5	5.5	6	6.5	7
Catalonia & Rest of Europe	38	38	39	39	40	41
USA	6	6.5	7	7.5	8	8.5

Barcelona's streets are not for faint-hearted drivers …

10 litres (17½ pt) of spirits and 90 litres (20 gall) of wine. If the goods are from duty free shops there is no limit to the quantity you can bring in. If you're coming to Spain from a country outside the EU, the limits are much more strict: 1 litre (1¾ pt) of spirits, 2 litres (3½ pt: a little over a bottle) of wine, 200 cigarettes and 50 cigars.

Driving

Driving is a good way to get around Catalonia, though it can be a nightmare in cities and in the twisted streets of tiny Catalan towns. If you do drive, be prepared for aggressive drivers who will be expecting you to drive with as much speed and daring as they do.

In all areas, peak traffic times are Friday evenings and Sunday evenings,

when all those who are heading out of town or returning from a weekend away clog the highways. The daily rush hours are 8–9.30am and 7–9pm.

Valid drivers' licences from most other countries (including the UK, US and Australia) are recognised in Catalonia if you're driving as a tourist.

Parking sign

... and they are not all as wide as this!

by phone or, when it's not peak season, by going directly to the agency's office and requesting a car. Nearly all cars in Catalonia are manual; if you require automatic transmission you'll almost certainly need to book in advance and will pay extra.

The main car rental agencies in Catalonia include Hertz (*www.hertz.com*), Europcar (*www.europcar.com*) and Avis (*www.avis.com*). All have offices at Barcelona's airport and at Barcelona's Sants rail station.

Non-EU citizens who are living in Spain need to obtain a Spanish drivers' licence.

Breakdowns

If you have car trouble or a breakdown, you can get help from RACC (*Tel: 902 106 106 or 902 307 307; www.racc.net*), the Catalan automobile club. If you belong to an automobile club in your home country ask about their emergency services abroad. You may be given a different number to call in case you need help (though regardless, you just might be attended by RACC).

Car hire

Numerous car hire firms operate in Catalonia. You can reserve a car online,

Fuel

There are petrol stations (*gasolineras*) up and down all major highways, and finding a place to fill up is not usually a problem. Leaded fuel (*gasolina*) and diesel (*diesel* or *gasoil*) are both sold; the latter is considerably cheaper. If you rent a car be sure to ask which type of fuel your vehicle requires.

Parking

The availability of parking depends greatly on where you are and what time of year it is. In the off season (usually winter), parking in most small towns on the coast or inland is easy. You'll usually be able to find a convenient parking spot, and more often than not it will be free.

Driving in peak season is another thing entirely. Finding a convenient, free parking space along the coast in July or August is nearly impossible. Unless you want to waste a morning driving in circles looking for an available spot, just budget for the price of a place in a car park (up to €20 a day).

In Barcelona you'll almost always have to pay for parking, with car parks charging €1.20 an hour and upwards. It's really best to leave your car outside the city, but if you must drive and park in Barcelona keep your eyes out for the large blue sign marked with a 'P'; this square street sign will point you to the nearest car park.

A word of caution: Catalonia multi-storey car parks are winding, cavernous places buried many metres underground, with the tiny spaces that can make it near-impossible for you to get out of your car.

Traffic regulations

Road signs in Catalonia follow EU standards, so most of them should be recognisable to drivers from other EU countries.

In Catalonia as in the rest of Spain, drivers drive on the right-hand side of the road. The far-right lane is reserved for slow vehicles, while the left lanes are for faster-moving traffic. It's very unsafe for a slow car to stay in the left lane. It is illegal to overtake on the right. If you come up to a slow car in the far left lane, that car is supposed to move over to let you pass. At crossroads, the car coming from the right always has the right of way, unless signposted differently. It is illegal to turn left to cross the solid central line

of a highway, even if you're turning into a petrol station, rest area or other establishment. Continue on until you find a place to turn around, then come back along the road and make a right turn into the establishment.

Speed limits are 120kph (75mph) on major highways, 80–90kph (50–56mph) on secondary highways and 50kph (31mph) in cities and towns. This is not strictly enforced, but Catalonia now has a system of camera patrols that ticket anyone going considerably over the speed limit. Permitted blood alcohol levels are extremely low in Catalonia compared to most other places in Europe. Breath checks are routine, especially in areas known for their nightlife.

The driver and front-seat passenger must wear seat belts. Children 12 and under cannot ride in the front seat, unless they're strapped into a special child's seat.

Keep your licence, vehicle registration and insurance papers in your car (or with you) at all times. You must carry a reflective jacket and safety reflectors in the car at all times.

Electricity

In Catalonia, as in the rest of Spain, the electric current is 220V. Electric plugs have two small round pins, like those in other parts of continental Europe. These pins are either thin (if it's an old appliance) or slightly fatter (newer appliance). Some of the humbler hotels and hostels still have the old-style plugs, so you may need to buy an adaptor.

Emergencies

If you have an emergency you can call the police on 091 or 092 from anywhere. For a medical emergency call 112 or for an ambulance 061. Catalonia has four different kinds of police: the municipal police, regional Catalan police (called Mossos d'Esquadra), the Guardia Civil and the National Police. Most crimes should be reported to the National Police (091).

Health

There aren't any particularly common health problems here, unless you count sunburn and hangovers, both of which are best cured with a bit of indoor rest and a lot of liquids. EU nationals with a European Health Insurance Card (EHIC) can consult a national health service doctor free of charge and any drugs prescribed can be bought at chemists at prices set by the Health Ministry. Nevertheless, adequate travel medical insurance is always advisable, and for non-EU citizens essential.

Pharmacies

Pharmacies are busy, useful places in Catalonia. Many drugs can be bought over the counter and the pharmacist has become an important figure in the health care chain. For minor medical problems you can simply explain your symptoms to the pharmacist and he or she will likely be able to help without your having to go to the doctor. Of course for important medical problems, go directly to a doctor.

Lost property

If you leave something at Barcelona's El Prat airport contact the airport

Compared with Barcelona's city streets, rural Catalonia can be a pleasure to drive in

Language

Catalan is similar to Spanish (*Castellano*), but it is definitely a language of its own with its own peculiarities. Like English, Catalan uses the unstressed 'uh' sound that appears in nearly every multi-syllable word. Thus 'how are you?', which is '¿Cómo estás?' in Spanish, with every vowel pronounced, becomes '¿Com estàs? in Catalan, with the first vowel in 'estàs' being an unstressed 'uh' sound. Consonants coming at the end of a word are often unpronounced. For example, *senyor* ('sir') is pronounced Sen-yoh, with no 'r' sound. 'V' is pronounced like a 'B', so *vostè* (the formal 'you') sounds like Boo-steh.

BASIC WORDS AND PHRASES

Hello	Hola
Goodbye	Adéu
Yes	Sí
No	No
Please	Sisplau
Thank you	Gràcies
You're welcome	De res
Do you speak English?	¿Vostè parla Angles?
I don't speak Catalan	No parlo Català.
Good day	Bon dia
Good evening	Bona nit
Excuse me	Perdoni
Sir	Senyor
Madam	Senyora
How are you?	¿Com està?
Very well, thank you	Molt bé, gràcies.
My name is...	Em dic…
What's your name?	¿Com et dius?
How do I get to...?	¿Per anar a...?
Where is...?	¿On és…?
The underground	El metro
The airport	L'aeroport
The train station	L'estació de tren
The bus	El bus
The street	El carrer
A taxicab	Un taxi
A hotel	Un hotel
The bathroom	El lavabo
A pharmacy	Una farmácia
A bank	un banc
The tourist office	L'oficina de turisme
What time is it?	Quina hora és?

EMERGENCIES

Help!	Socors!
I am sick	Em trobo malament
I am hurt	Estic ferit/ferida
The hospital	L'hospital
A doctor	Un metge

DAYS AND MONTHS

Monday	Dilluns
Tuesday	Dimarts
Wednesday	Dimecres
Thursday	Dijous
Friday	Divendres
Saturday	Dissabte
Sunday	Diumenge
January	Gener
February	Febrer
March	Març
April	Abril
May	Maig
June	Juny
July	Juliol
August	Agost
September	Setembre
October	Octubre
November	Novembre
December	Desembre

NUMBERS

Zero	Zero	**Six**	Sis
One	Un/Una	**Seven**	Set
Two	Dos/Dues	**Eight**	Vuit
Three	Tres	**Nine**	Nou
Four	Quatre	**Ten**	Deu
Five	Cinc		

information desk immediately (*Tel: 93 298 3838*). Elsewhere, contact local police to enquire about lost property procedures.

Maps

Many companies publish maps of Catalonia. One of the best and most readily available is Michelin's 574 regional map of Aragón and Catalonia. This is a great highway map that shows enough detail to allow you to explore off the main highways. Michelin also does an excellent, detailed Barcelona map available in booklet or traditional broadsheet format. Locally printed Distrimaps are also good and especially useful is their Catalunya Comarques map that divides the region into counties for easy orientation.

Public holidays

There are more than two dozen public holidays in Catalonia, and that doesn't count the local festivals and feast days that are taken as additional holidays in many towns. When a holiday falls on a Thursday or a Tuesday, people often take what's called a *puente* (bridge), claiming the Friday or Monday as a holiday too and taking a 4-day break from work. On these weekends, you're nearly guaranteed traffic jams on all highways leading to the beaches or the mountains.

The following is a list of public holidays in Catalonia. For more on festivals, *see pp22–3*.

1 Jan New Year's Day
6 Jan Three Kings' Day
Mar/Apr Good Friday, Easter Sunday and Easter Monday
1 May Labour Day
May/June Second Easter Monday (Barcelona only)
24 June St John the Baptist's Day
15 Aug Feast of the Assumption
11 Sept National Day of Catalonia
24 Sept Festival of La Mercé (Barcelona only)
12 Oct National Day of Spain

Most street signs are in Catalan rather than Spanish

Barcelona's metro system is supplemented by a dense bus network

8 Dec Feast of the Immaculate
Conception
25 Dec Christmas Day
26 Dec St Stephen's Day

Public transport

Moving around by train is easy with
the extensive RENFE (*www.renfe.es*)
network. All large towns and cities
have railway stations, as do many
tourist destinations like Montserrat and
the Port Aventura theme park. To reach
smaller towns and out-of-the-way
destinations without a car, you'll need
to take a bus. Main regional bus
companies in Catalonia include:
Alsina Graells (*Tel: 93 265 6866;
www.alsinagraells.net*), buses to
Pyrenees.
Casas (*Tel: 93 798 1100*), buses to many
coastal resorts.

Hife (*Tel: 93 322 7814*), buses to
southern Catalonia.
Hispania (*Tel: 93 231 2756*), buses to
southern and central Catalonia.
Sagalés (*Tel: 90 213 0014;
www.sagales.com*), buses to central
Catalonia.
Sarfa (*Tel: 90 230 2025; www.sarfa.es*),
buses to the Costa Brava.
Teisa (*Tel: 97 220 4868;
www.teisa-bus.com*), buses to
Pre-Pyrenees.

In Barcelona, the major bus station is
the Estació Nord (*Carrer d'Alí Bei 80,
Tel: 93 265 6508*).

Sustainable tourism

Thomas Cook is a strong advocate of
ethical and fairly traded tourism and
believes that the travel experience
should be as good for the places visited

as it is for the people who visit them. That's why we firmly support The Travel Foundation, a charity that develops solutions to help improve and protect holiday destinations, their environment, traditions and culture. To find out what you can do to make a positive difference to the places you travel to and the people who live there, please visit *www.thetravelfoundation.org.uk*

Taxis

Taxis are plentiful and useful in Barcelona; the minimum fare is €1.30. Hailing a taxi is usually not a problem, even at night. If you need to call for one, ring 93 303 3033. A taxi from the airport to central Barcelona will cost about €20, but taxis from the airport to other towns will cost considerably more, especially if you have to travel on toll highways. In smaller towns taxi stands tend to be near the railway stations, and although prices are usually incredibly high considering the short distances, this may be the easiest way to get from the station to your hotel.

Tipping is not obligatory, but most drivers appreciate it if you simply round up the fare.

Telephones

To dial Spain from abroad, first dial your local international code, then dial 34 and the nine-digit number. If you're calling from within Spain to another country, first dial 00 then dial the country code (for example,

44 for the UK and 1 for the US) and the phone number.

Within Spain, you must dial all nine digits of the phone number. Land lines begin with 9, while mobile phone numbers begin with 6.

Tipping

See p27.

Toilets

Public toilets are a rarity, which means that you'll probably have to use the facilities at a bar or restaurant. Most establishments are kind enough to let you quickly use the loo even if you've just walked in off the street, but the proper thing to do is to first buy a coffee or water and then head to the bathroom.

Tourist information

Each town has its own municipal tourist office where you can find

Phone boxes are stylish and hard to miss

The Barcelona Metro

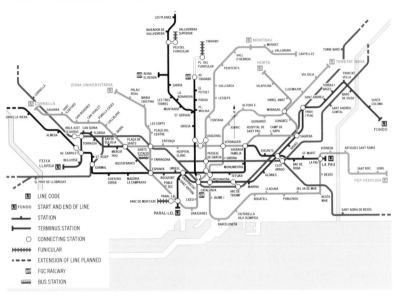

L1	LINE CODE
L1 FONDO	START AND END OF LINE
	STATION
	TERMINUS STATION
○	CONNECTING STATION
++++++	FUNICULAR
= = = =	EXTENSION OF LINE PLANNED
	FGC RAILWAY
	BUS STATION

information about local culture, events and attractions. These little offices can be invaluable resources for finding out the best things to see and do in a

Tourist information office, Barcelona

place. They're also good sources of information about public holidays and festivals, accommodation and restaurants. The main Catalan tourist office is in Barcelona at the intersection of Avinguda Diagonal and Rambla de Catalunya. There you'll find a wealth of information about the region and all it has to offer. The office's website is *www.gencat.net/probert* or *www.catalunyaturisme.net*

Travellers with disabilities

Though access to public buildings and transportation is slowly improving, it still has a long way to go before Catalonia is equally accessible to all. Be sure to ask before booking a hotel room if there are good entry ramps and if there are disability-adapted rooms.

Index

Acknowledgements

Thomas Cook wishes to thank the photographers, picture libraries and other organisations for the loan of the photographs reproduced in this book, to whom copyright in the photographs belongs.

EL BULLI PRESS/Francesc Guillamet 112, 113; FURA PRESS 154, 155; JOSEP CANO 68, 70, 128, 129, 131b, 142, 143; FLICKR/Xavier Cabelle 69, Horitzons Inesperats 86; FORUM PRESS OFFICE 33; FOTOLIA/Ian Ferguson 15, Randi Utnes 20, L@gui 25, Horst Voigt 36, Ralph Kretschmer 57, Andrea Seamann 147; HOTEL PRESS 173, 175; IBERIMAGES 142; PICTURES COLOUR LIBRARY 26, 32, 84, 147, 152, 159; NEIL SETCHFIELD 5, 152; VIAS VERDES PRESS 107; WIKIMEDIA COMMONS/anon 8, Zaqarbal 14, Nathan Badera 41, Yearofthedragon 47, anon 71a, G M Kowalewska 73, David Mateos García 109, anon 117; WORLD PICTURES/Photoshot 1, 21, 27, 29, 30, 40, 45, 48, 49, 85, 102, 141, 145, 161.

All other photographs were taken by SARAH ANDREWS.

Proofreading: Ian Faulkner for CAMBRIDGE PUBLISHING MANAGEMENT LTD

SEND YOUR THOUGHTS TO
BOOKS@THOMASCOOK.COM

We're committed to providing the very best up-to-date information in our travel guides and constantly strive to make them as useful as they can be. You can help us to improve future editions by letting us have your feedback. If you've made a wonderful discovery on your travels that we don't already feature, if you'd like to inform us about recent changes to anything that we do include, or if you simply want to let us know your thoughts about this guidebook and how we can make it even better – we'd love to hear from you.

Send us ideas, discoveries and recommendations today and then look out for your valuable input in the next edition of this title. And, as an extra 'thank you' from Thomas Cook Publishing, you'll be automatically entered into our exciting prize draw.

Emails to the above address, or letters to Travellers Project Editor, Thomas Cook Publishing, PO Box 227, Coningsby Road, Peterborough PE3 8SB, UK.

Please don't forget to let us know which title your feedback refers to!